Information Technology for Learning: No School Left Behind

by Ferdi C. Serim

Janet Murray, Editor

Information Technology for Learning: No School Left Behind

by Ferdi C. Serim

This publication is available from
Big6 Associates, LLC
P. O. Box 388
Ashland, OH 44805
800-247-6553
419-281-1802 (international)
419-281-6883 (fax)

ISBN: 0-9725391-0-7

Published by Big6 Associates, LLC
P. O. Box 1, Fayetteville, NY 13066
www.big6.org
info@big6.com

Lloyd Lathrop, Designer

Ferdi Serim helps people learn to read, write and think, using technology to expand the boundaries of what they read, write and think about. His work as board member of the Consortium for School Networking (CoSN), director of the Online Internet Institute (OII), Associate of the David Thornburg Center for Professional Development (and jazz musician) helps people understand and harness technology's transforming potentials for distributed learning and networked knowing. He is the author of *NetLearning: Why Teachers Use the Internet* (published by Songline, a division of O'Reilly and Associates) and *From Computers to Community: Unlocking the Potentials of the Wired Classroom* (published by Centrinity Incorporated). His goal is to help people move from vision to strategy, increasing the opportunities for learning, for everyone.

Ferdi has walked the talk: his students' Internet achievements are documented in the *Scientific American*, *Los Angeles Times*, the Learning Channel and other media. Ferdi is a founder of the Online Internet Institute <http://oii.org>, which was started with funding by the National Science Foundation. OII is committed to reshaping the nature of teaching and learning by helping educators, students and parents use the Internet to improve achievement in the classroom, and beyond. OII provides the tools for people to learn, interact and grow in ways necessary for the 21st Century.

Ferdi also presents at numerous state, regional and international conferences, conducts staff development workshops and seminars for parents, teachers, school administrators and others involved in systemic school reform, including the US Department of Education, National Science Foundation, the Milken Exchange on Educational Technology, the Singapore and Malaysia ministries of education, and others. Ferdi is a member of the advisory board for the Digital Divide Clearinghouse, and WNET's Internet in Action telecourse on professional development. His favorite credential, however, comes from Dizzy Gillespie, who said he's a "pretty good drummer."

contents

List of Worksheets

There is nothing more exciting than seeing students approach what they thought was a limit, and then take ownership of new learning as they watch the challenge recede in the rear view mirror. Once they are moving, once they are encouraged, learners become bolder. With each success, they expand both their world and the roles they can choose to play in this world.

There is nothing more tragic than a dream deferred. Whether the dream comes from a student's curiosity or a teacher's desire, dreams have a limited shelf life before going nowhere makes them fade away. For too many students and teachers, information technology has been a dream deferred because it has been neither adequately understood, nor adequately supported.

There is nothing more powerful than collaboration in transforming dreams into realities. Although my path as an educator taught me this long ago, writing this book has convinced me of this more than ever. This book is living proof of the power of Information & Technology (I&T) teams. Writing it required one.

In the pages that follow, you'll see much about teamwork, and how five key roles need to be performed in order to improve learning in the 21st century. When I say "we" in this book, there are real people, not roles, behind the words and ideas. At the center is partnership.

The reality of how learning improves when we are willing (and know how) to learn from each other, support one another, challenge one another as we work together toward a shared vision over time has been illustrated in the development of this book.

Not Deferred, Not a Dream: I&T Teams

A decade ago, five centuries after Columbus' voyage of encounter, the 21st century arrived in my classroom, with our first connection to the Internet. At that time, I met Janet Murray, who I already knew had been one of the builders of the first global network for kids, one which preceded the Internet.

You see her name as editor, but in reality, she is a co-creator of the bridges that lead from vision to strategy in this book.

What we shared then, we still share: awe at what students can do when they have both traditional and contemporary literacy to rely upon as they navigate their way from school into life. The most important of these are conceptual skills that help them to apply their learning to solving problems, in school, in work, at home.

Of course, most of what I needed to know in order to best help my students had been left out of my training as a teacher: I hadn't gone to library school. The fact that I didn't encounter computers was insignificant compared to the absence of guidance in understanding that information's power depended on how it was organized, viewed and applied. Because Janet Murray is a teacher, as well as an information specialist, we built bridges between the worlds of classroom instruction and library/media learning. Janet is the reason it was easy for me to come up with the image of Scholar used in this book.

While the arrival of information technology forever changed the way I teach and learn, the schools in which we work remain largely unchanged. As enormous a change as the arrival of the Internet may be, it pales in comparison with the change that happened with the passage of the ESEA *No Child Left Behind* Act. Coming two decades after *A Nation At Risk* (Gardner) the education landscape will be profoundly altered by the shift of focus away from "inputs" and onto student results. However, these changes also come at a time when we must decide whether or not our purpose is to prepare students (and ourselves) for 21st century learning. This book prepares every school to move ahead, in order to move every child ahead.

These observations are not conceptual for me; they are visceral. I began teaching in Newark, NJ in 1973, in a building six years older than the Statue of Liberty. Since then, I've become the poster child for five careers in one lifetime. After six years as a systems analyst in two engineering companies, I returned to education as a middle school computer teacher. This district was a showcase, and had a district technology coordinator, library/media specialists and computer teachers in each school, and technicians who did troubleshooting and in-house repair that kept most of our gear working. It was the way things should be, but aren't, for too many schools in our nation.

In the past decade, I've consulted with thousands of teachers in hundreds of schools in districts and states across the nation, as well as working with educators internationally. The only thing that has advanced more quickly than the technology's power and affordability has been the complexity of challenges facing education as an institution. This book is about hope, not fear. Hope is an appropriate response to complexities we face, because they force us to work at a higher level: collaboration. Anyone who's taken on the task of managing technology in schools quickly comes to the same conclusion: this job is too big for me!

The secret is: this job is too big for anyone. The job requires the skills that are normally found in four people, to provide management of relationships, information, instruction and resources. We invite you to experience the power of I&T teams as a strategy for 21st century learning!

Ferdi Serim
Santa Fe, NM May 2003

acknowledgements

This book is truly the result of communication and collaboration among a Dream Team comprised of information and technology leaders, visionaries and innovators. Without the support and encouragement from Mike Eisenberg, Bob Berkowitz, Sue Wurster and the rest of the Big6 family, this book would have never come into being, and certainly never have achieved the level of quality that we strove for. As a musician, I'd have to thank Dizzy Gillespie and Charlie Parker for inventing bebop; as an educator, in the same spirit I thank Mike and Bob for inventing the Big6.

I've been blessed with mentors too. David Thornburg has been a constant guiding star, and I'm nourished by his thoughts and our conversations about the way Contemporary Literacy plays a defining role as we shape the future. And Mike Eisenberg, beyond first expressing the need for I&T teams in his "call to action," along with Jamie McKenzie, convinced me to go out on my own, and make my work more widely available…I'm continually grateful for the inspiration they provide.

Similarly, over the past few years, I've deepened my relationships with the talented individuals I've met on the Consortium for School Networking Board. Keith Krueger, Bob Moore, Jim Hirsch, Jim Bosco, Marla Davenport, Andy Carvin, Shirley Smith and Helen Soule have all contributed to crafting the vision expressed in this book. This work has also allowed me to work alongside great spirits including Don Knezek, Cheryl Williams, Dean Bergman, Linda Roberts, Chris Dede, Margaret Riel, Jason Ravitz, Allan Olson, Jenny House, Mona Westhaver, Kathleen Fulton, John Vaille and Paul Pruess. Talk about a Dream Team!

The OII family is another source of strength for this work. Art Wolinsky has seen more than his share of conference rooms, hotel rooms and workshop rooms with me, yet whenever we get together, we pursue the same conversation: how good learning could be, and how could we make this happen for more people? Janet Murray has educated all of us about the importance of information literacy so powerfully that advancing the cause of Contemporary Literacy is at the core of all we do. Celia Einhorn and Betsy Frederick continually remind us that the world is larger than the USA, and that global collaboration among the young is our best hope for the future.

My own family has nobly borne the weight of sacrifices required to complete this work. Joey, my wife, has endured weeks where I placed myself in the "witless protection program" and experienced the consequences of accepting too many irresistible projects. As a teacher of special needs children for nearly three decades, she has tuned my thinking about reaching every child, about balancing technology with the need for humanizing influences, and about having a giving heart. My son Ari and daughter Jasmin lived with this project for three of our final summers together before striking out on their own. Beyond being gifted and giving human beings, they reassure me about the difference 21st century literacy can make in terms of the life choices one has available. I am grateful for the wonderful blessings all these relationships provide in my life and work.

Ferdi Serim

"The only limits are, as always, those of vision."

— *James Broughton*

"Research and practice have demonstrated the important role that vision and mission play in organizations - especially schools... Both formal and informal leaders communicate their vision by how they spend their time, what they talk about, what problems they solve first, and what they get excited about. In every act, leaders reinforce the values they hold and the vision they hope to achieve." (Develop)

Perhaps the most important ingredient in educational technology today is **vision**. Leadership with vision is focused, avoids the waves of educational fads, and initiates internal improvement. With a consistent vision guiding a school's direction, it is possible to create effective programs whose implementation will survive the departure of a particular administrator.

Information Technology for Learning details our vision of contemporary literacy and a strategy for making the journey from this vision to practice. Chapter One defines contemporary literacy, and the remainder of the book focuses on how to achieve this vision through the efforts of key educators working together as part of **Information & Technology (I&T) Teams**. The members of the I&T Team are the people in schools who are most involved in the implementation of technology: the principal, the library media specialist, the teacher leader and the technical specialist (supported by the District Technology Coordinator). Chapter Three describes the roles of these key people; Chapter Four guides their dialogues; and Chapter Five provides resources to inform their efforts. Worksheets to facilitate assembling and guiding your I&T team appear at strategic points throughout the book.

Chapter One
Our Vision: The Importance of Contemporary Literacy in the Digital Age

"Vision without action is a daydream. Action without vision is a nightmare."
— Japanese Proverb

Vision doesn't exist in a vacuum. Instead, vision leads to a destination that is so compelling it can be explained and understood in common sense terms. The vision that drives this book is contemporary literacy.

Technology is the Big Bang that has propelled traditional literacy (i.e., reading and writing) into an expanded universe of literacies. "**Information Technology (IT)**" is the phrase commonly used to refer to the complex interactions now possible between computer networks and the massive amounts of data they can generate and process.

Technology extends traditional literacy by enabling people to perceive relationships hidden below the surface of vast amounts of data, and to synthesize meaning from these relationships. The challenge to comprehend rapidly expanding technology requires a new "contemporary literacy." However, contemporary literacy involves far more than **information technology literacy** alone; our vision of contemporary literacy embraces not only computers and data, but the critical thinking skills required to use them effectively.

Chapter Two
Leading from Vision to Practice

"Leadership is the capacity to translate vision into reality.

— *Warren G. Bennis*

In *Information Technology for Learning*, we advocate a shared-leadership model, founded on the **Information & Technology (I&T) Team**. We cannot raise student achievement through levitation. It takes hard, sustained, coordinated work. Our alchemy depends on blending individual talents into teams.

What we know: when people collaborate, they multiply exponentially the power of their ideas, experiences and intentions. The nostalgic image of the inventor toiling in a workshop has been replaced by collaborative workgroups, often numbering in the hundreds. The most recent upgrade of any software you use today is likely to have required hundreds of thousands of hours of work. A team of ten programmers can accomplish this upgrade in five years. A team of 100 programmers can do the same in six months.

Chapter Three
Leadership Roles: Which Hats Do You Wear?

The reality in far too many schools leaves someone feeling like a one-man band. Staffing hasn't increased to meet the demands of teaching and learning in a digital age. In Chapter Three, we examine the roles required to build and sustain an effective information technology program, one that adds value

Information Technology for Learning: No School Left Behind

Our Vision: Contemporary Literacy in the Digital Age

- Building on Traditional Literacies
- Expanding the Definition of Literacy
- Ensuring Student Mastery in Information Technology
- Achieving Contemporary Literacy

Leading from Vision to Practice

- From Promise to Practice: The Big6 Skills
- From Vision to Strategy: The Information & Technology Team
- Strong Medicine: Scientifically Based Research, School Practice and Accountability
- Flying Blind? 21st Century Navigation Tools for Improved Learning

Leadership Roles: Which Hats Do You Wear?

- **Wizard**
  - Chief Technology Officer
  - District Tech Coordinator
- **Pilot**
  - Building Level Principal
- **Scholar**
  - Library Media Specialist
- **Guide**
  - Teacher Leader
- **HardHat**
  - Building Level Technical Specialist

Key Conversations: How I&T Teams Manage Change

- **Accountability:**
  - Pilot
  - Scholar
  - Guide
- **Learning:**
  - Wizard
  - Scholar
  - Guide
  - HardHat
- **Leadership:**
  - Wizard
  - Pilot
  - Scholar
- **Technical:**
  - Wizard
  - Pilot
  - Scholar
  - HardHat

Team Resources: Vision into Practice

- **Accountability:** Making IT Work for Assessment and Growth
- **Learning:** Harnessing the Power of IT
- **Leadership:** Making IT Work to Provide Sustained Support
- **Technical:** Making IT Work for Everyone!

to all parts of the system. As you read these descriptions, think of how many of these hats you wear, and who might be ready to wear hats that aren't being worn (but need to be) in your building. This will be an important first step to forming your I&T Team.

The first section, *Defining the Roles*, should be read by everyone, in order to understand the talents and experience the person playing each role brings to your team.

The second section, *Wearing the Hats*, should be consulted whenever you need more detail and guidance about playing any particular role.

Chapter Four
Key Conversations: How I&T Teams Manage Change

The power of I&T Teams comes from the potential to focus upon a common vision, to address building level challenges in implementing new literacies - particularly the essential information and technology skills and knowledge defined and articulated in Chapter One. Successful implementation of information and technology skills and knowledge requires initiating new conversations among people who don't usually collaborate in a sustained or organized way. Chapter Four provides the prompts to begin these conversations, as you expand awareness and implementation of contemporary literacy beyond your I&T Team, to embrace the entire school community. The insights you will gain about the skills and talents found on your team, as well as ways you can help each other face challenges you used to face alone, will build the foundation for sustainable, building level support.

Chapter Five
Team Resources: Vision into Practice

The resources in *Information Technology for Learning* are purposefully organized in the following way: **Accountability, Learning, Leadership and Technical**. Here's why:

Accountability measures are already in place, which schools are required to address right now. Period.

Learning in the 21st century goes far beyond the "cutoff score" design of accountability measures, as well as the capabilities of measurement tools. We must design for this higher standard, to properly serve every child and strengthen every school.

Leadership's first priority is to decide how to accomplish these closely related goals, by assembling the support, resources and civic participation to make your school a place where learning demonstrably exceeds accountability performance goals.

Technical decisions cannot be made until these three required elements are in place. This means looking at your technology infrastructure in three ways. How can learning be strengthened by proper use of what you have now? What's the life cycle for your current resources? What's your plan for refreshing your infrastructure as new educational benefits become clear?

Information Technology for Learning shows in clear, practical language how to connect your human and technology resources for success. By forming Information & Technology (I&T) Teams at the building level, incorporating the Big6™ Skills (a proven information-based problem solving process), and harnessing the power of technology to support good teaching, good learning becomes possible for everyone: students, teachers, administrators and the community.

chapter 1

Our Vision:

**Contemporary Literacy
in the Digital Age**

1.1 Overview

The demands of our 21st Century society
are stretching schools (and school people) to
the breaking point. Schools are, rightfully,
being asked to focus on achieving academic
success for every student, to leave no child
behind (*No Child Left Behind*). As I
researched and prepared a series of white
papers for the Consortium for School
Networking (COSN) on topics of vital
concern related to the demands of NCLB
(Scientifically Based Research, Data-Driven
Decision-Making and Accountability), I
discovered that, for the most part, this
worthy aim is being translated into more
detailed explications of curriculum goals
and objectives (as state and local standards
or frameworks) and more frequent and
elaborate testing.

More is not necessarily better - in terms of curriculum standards or testing - and more certainly will not guarantee student success.

To us, achieving academic success for all students centers not on outlining more curriculum, but instead on redefining the fundamentals of education as embodied in the central and essential concept of "literacy." We call this, "contemporary literacy." Infusing contemporary literacy in learning and teaching is the heart of our vision for education in the 21st Century.

Contemporary Literacy does, of course, include the fundamental skills of reading and writing text. However, contemporary literacy also includes technology and information-based problem solving skills.

In this chapter, we define and explore contemporary literacy by addressing the following questions:

- What roles do traditional literacies (reading, writing, arithmetic) play?
- How has the definition of literacy been expanded by the realities of the digital age? What computer or information technology skills and knowledge does contemporary literacy encompass?
- How can we help our students achieve contemporary literacy?

1.2 Building on Traditional Literacies:
Excerpt from "Contemporary Literacy: Essential Skills for the 21st Century"

Traditionally, schools taught the "three R's: reading, 'riting and 'rithmetic." *Literacy* was captured in international census data by estimating the percentage of people who could read and write.

As computers became essential in the workplace and dribbled into schools, *computer literacy* entered the curriculum, usually in the form of an introduction to the new vocabulary of bits and bytes, hardware and software. Computer courses focused on programming languages. "Keyboarding" replaced typing.

The term *information literacy* first appeared in the mid-1970s as awareness grew that information was becoming an overwhelming and unmanageable deluge. In the 1980s, people realized that computers might be useful tools for organizing and retrieving information. In 1989, the American Library

Association codified a definition which provided the basis for subsequent discussion: "To be information literate, a person must be able to recognize when information is needed and have the ability to locate, evaluate, and use effectively the needed information." (Final Report) In other words, *literacy* implies more than vocabulary and awareness; it requires critical thinking.

This connotation of *literacy* - one that includes interpretation and evaluation of a medium of expression - has been applied in many different contexts. We read about visual literacy, media literacy, textual literacy, numerical literacy, technology literacy and network literacy. In each case, the author expects the word *literacy* to suggest a complex of skills, including analysis, evaluation, synthesis and application. (Murray, Contemporary Literacy)

The American Association of School Librarians collaborated with the Association for Educational Communications and Technology (AECT) to codify national "Information Literacy Standards for Student Learning." This powerful collection of nine standards and 29 indicators of proficiency in information literacy, independent learning and socially responsible use of electronic information can provide the foundation for organizing interdisciplinary research activities that promote critical thinking and the acquisition of the information processing skills necessary for future success.

Our vision of contemporary literacy both incorporates information literacy and builds upon traditional literacy. Reading is still fundamental, whether from printed paper, a screen, or some new digital form. But students must also be able to process information in visual, aural, video, and all kinds of combinations of multimedia forms. Writing is also an essential skill for success. Students must still write, although it is much more effective and efficient to do so using word processing technology. For example, Rockman ET AL (2000) found that students with regular access to laptop computers were stronger than their peers in four areas of writing: content, organization, language/voice/style, and mechanics. And, students will certainly need to be able to express and present their ideas in other formats as well, using technologies yet to be developed.

1.2.1 Research Basis for Information Literacy

In her recent literature review of the extensive research basis for an information literacy approach, Carrie Lowe, information specialist with the Public Broadcasting System, writes, "The existing body of research on information literacy can be considered in the context of three themes, which are the nature and scope of information literacy, the value of information literacy, and effective methods of information literacy skills instruction." (Lowe)

On the nature and scope of information literacy, Lowe notes "[C.C.] Kuhlthau's research contributions led to a much greater understanding of the importance of teaching information skills (such as individual steps in The Big6) in context and not as discrete tasks. Kuhlthau's (1993) research into the information seeking behavior of students contributed to her central philosophy of information literacy - that information literacy is not a set of individual tasks or skills, but rather a way of thinking that allows individuals to be the flexible thinkers and lifelong learners who will succeed in the information age."

Regarding the value of information literacy, Lowe notes that the cognitive aspects and related benefits are key. "Pitts' (1995) examination of the mental models of students engaged in the information problem-solving process found that they use different domains of knowledge to complete a task, including one responsible for information seeking and use and others related to the other aspects of the task, including subject knowledge. Pitts found that a lack of knowledge in one area (including information problem-solving skills) could limit learning and success overall." (Lowe)

1.3 Expanding the Definition of Literacy

How have the realities of the digital age caused us to expand our definition of literacy?

The Bertelsmann Foundation and the AOL Time Warner Foundation joined with experts from education, business and government to convene an international 21st Century Literacy Summit in March 2002. The summit further expanded the definition of contemporary literacy to incorporate more than *information literacy* and *computer literacy*. The White Paper resulting from that conference concludes:

The explosive growth of technology in every aspect of society offers us a unique opportunity to engage our citizens in economic and civic life. Digital technologies have given us new and better ways to teach and learn. They have made us more efficient at work. And they are enabling us to participate more directly in the governance of our lives...In return, they demand that we continually acquire and develop new knowledge and skills. Information and communication technologies are raising the bar on the competencies needed to succeed in the 21st century, and they are compelling us to revisit many of our assumptions and beliefs. (White Paper)

1.4 Ensuring Student Mastery in Information Technology

The 1999 National Research Council report *Being Fluent with Information Technology* is the most comprehensive and forward-thinking treatment of information technology (IT) literacy. This report notes that

> Fluency with information technology requires three kinds of knowledge: contemporary skills, foundational concepts, and intellectual capabilities.

- **Contemporary skills**, the ability to use today's computer applications, enable people to apply information technology immediately. In the present labor market, skills are an essential component of job readiness. Most importantly, skills provide a store of practical experience on which to build new competence.
- **Foundational concepts**, the basic principles and ideas of computers, networks, and information, underpin the technology. Concepts explain the how and why of information technology, and they give insight into its opportunities and limitations. Concepts are the raw material for understanding new information technology as it evolves.
- **Intellectual capabilities**, the ability to apply information technology in complex and sustained situations, encapsulate higher-level thinking

in the context of information technology. Capabilities empower people to manipulate the medium to their advantage and to handle unintended and unexpected problems when they arise. The intellectual capabilities foster more abstract thinking about information and its manipulation. (Executive Summary, Being Fluent)

1.4.1 Defining and Measuring IT Literacy

Only when the people responsible for curricular, instructional, management and technical aspects of the school operate from a shared understanding of the importance of **Information Technology (IT) Literacy** (or Information and Communications Technology (ICT)Literacy) can their actions align to

IT Taxonomy Inventory: Media for Inquiry, Communication, Construction, and Expression

"A taxonomy can be a productive step in the process of understanding and explaining what we see by organizing perceptions into categories if we are able to see the familiar in new ways or if we are able to cope with a confusing array of phenomena." Bruce and Levin built their taxonomy "not on a formal instructional model, nor on hardware and software features, but rather, on the 'impulses' to learn and grow" in an attempt to identify instructional uses for technology that their colleagues had not considered. Rather than focus on tools, they advocate examining uses, which generates an approach that allows us to more meaningfully integrate technology as a way of extending learning.

A. Media for Inquiry	Examples
1. Theory building—technology as media for thinking.	Model exploration/ simulation toolkits; Visualization software; Knowledge representation
2. Data access—connecting to the world of texts, video, data	Hypertext and hypermedia environments; Library access (including digital libraries, databases; Music, voice, images, graphics, video, data tables, graphs, text
3. Data collection—using technology to extend the senses	Remote scientific instruments accessible via networks; Microcomputer-based laboratories, with sensors for temperature, motion, heart rate, etc.; Survey makers for student-run surveys and interviews; Video and sound recording
4. Data analysis	Exploratory data analysis; Statistical analysis; Environments for inquiry; Image processing; Spreadsheets; Programs to make tables and graphs; Problem-solving programs

B. Media for Communication	Examples
1. Document preparation	Word processing; Outlining; Graphics; Spelling, grammar, usage, and style aids; Symbolic expressions; Desktop publishing; Presentation graphics
2. Communication—with other students, teachers, experts, and people worldwide	E-mail; Asynchronous and Synchronous computer conferencing (text, audio, video, etc.); web servers; Student-created hypertext environments
3. Collaborative Media	Collaborative data environments; Group decision support systems; Shared document preparation
4. Teaching Media	Tutoring systems; Instructional simulations; Drill and practice systems; Telementoring

C. Media for Construction	Examples
Control systems—using technology to affect the physical world	Robotics, Control of equipment; Computer-aided design; Construction of graphs and charts

D. Media for Expression	Examples
Exploring, inventing and experiencing the world.	Drawing and painting programs; Music making and accompaniment; Music composing and editing; Interactive video and hypermedia; Animation software; Multimedia composition

Bruce and Levin

make contemporary literacy possible for all students. In *Digital Transformation: A Framework for ICT Literacy*, Educational Testing Service (ETS) gathered a distinguished panel of international researchers, who found that

> ICT literacy cannot be defined primarily as the mastery of technical skills... the concept of ICT literacy should be broadened to include both critical cognitive skills as well as the application of technical skills and knowledge. These cognitive skills include general literacy, such as reading and numeracy, as well as critical thinking and problem solving. Without such skills, the panel believes that true ICT literacy cannot be attained. (Digital Transformation)

Given the new national educational policy focus on improving student achievement, through research-based practices that document student growth, the work to build IT assessments is both timely and imperative. As noted in the 1999 National Research Council report *Being Fluent with Information Technology*, the

> requirement of a deeper understanding than is implied by the rudimentary term "computer literacy" motivated the committee to adopt "fluency" as a term connoting a higher level of competency. People fluent with information technology (FIT persons) are able to express themselves creatively, to reformulate knowledge, and to synthesize new information. Fluency with information technology (i.e., what this report calls FITness) entails a process of lifelong learning in which individuals continually apply what they know to adapt to change and acquire more knowledge to be more effective at applying information technology to their work and personal lives.(Being Fluent)

The goal of developing measures of these skills needs to recognize both the context, as well as the nature of the process, and how this process differs from those typically measured in schools. The report notes, "Because FITness is fundamentally integrative, calling upon an individual to coordinate information and skills with respect to multiple dimensions of a problem and to make overall judgments and decisions taking all such information into account, a project-based approach to developing FITness is most appropriate." (Being Fluent)

1.5 Achieving Contemporary Literacy

How do the new literacies require us to shift from traditional practice?

To illustrate the changes required, I'll resort to a musical analogy to make the point. As a jazz musician, I thrive on freedom. I can play anything I desire to express almost any musical situation. The ability to "sit in" with other musicians from other genres is one of the most rewarding aspects of this approach.

However, this freedom comes only after years of practicing the fundamentals of tone, time and timbre. When we skip to the progressive, creative level without providing the foundation upon which these skills depend, we do so at our own peril. At best, we get music that's more fun to play than it is to listen to!

In music we have three levels of progression:

- **Fundamentals** - when you learn to play your instrument, learn where the notes are and how to produce them, learn rhythm, harmony, and notation.
- **Performance** - when you learn the literature appropriate to the time and place of your culture. In western classical music, you'll play Bach, Beethoven, Schubert, maybe even a little Debussy...in rock music, you'll learn the blues, and maybe even some music from before you were born. Learning by doing is the key to this phase.
- **Creative** - when you begin to apply what you've learned to create expressions that didn't exist before, whether these be jazz improvisations, arrangements or orchestrations of other composer's works, new settings for poems or sound tracks for movies. You begin to synthesize all that you've heard, all that you've done, all that you've discovered into sounds that may be the result of individual or group collaborative efforts.

In education, there are three distinctive approaches:

- **The Traditional** - when we only ask questions to which the answers are already known. This is the "transmission" model of teaching.
- **The Progressive** - when the process is as important as the product. This is the "show your work" model, where the thinking processes that led students to an answer provides a window into their reasoning, understanding and comprehension.

• **The Transformative** - the application of what's been learned in the authentic context of meaningful activity that deepens and strengthens learning. The keyword "purposeful" describes activities done at this level, as in genuine WebQuests, which result in the construction of new knowledge.

No one would think of passing out tubes and telling kids "punch some holes in these tubes wherever you'd like, and create your own musical vocabulary" implying there was no such thing as notes, scales or chords. While it might be fun as a project in the physics of acoustics, it doesn't make sense for learning to play music.

Yet some people think that we can skip these fundamentals when we place computers in the hands of kids and teachers, who most likely have neither the conceptual nor procedural tools to guide their efforts. We've moved our focus from media literacy to computer literacy to information literacy without having assured either basic literacy or consideration of what is meant by the contemporary literacy that is required to function as a member of today's world.

Framing the discussion in terms of contemporary literacy, while honoring the three stages required to move learners of any age as far as they can go, is a good strategy for implementing technology in the curriculum. By doing so, we can prepare each teacher to see the value of their contributions to moving students ahead on a path that merits the name "lifelong."

1.5.1 Expanding from Traditional Practice

What models can guide us in moving from promise to practice?

In December 2000, the U.S. Department of Education released the second National Technology Plan. Addressing contemporary literacy, *e-Learning: Putting a World Class Education at the Fingertips of All Children* states "A meaningful, unified approach to providing students with the skills they will need for their futures must be more than a checklist of isolated technology skills, such as knowing the parts of a computer, writing drafts and final products with a word processor, or searching for information using a CD-ROM database."

Rather, technology skills are only a first step in assuring all our children become proficient information and technology users. Also necessary are information literacy skills such as:

- **Task Definition** - The first step in the information problem-solving process is to recognize that an information need exists, to define the problem, and to identify the types and extent of information needed.
- **Information Seeking Strategies** - Once the information problem has been formulated, the student must consider all possible information sources and develop a plan for searching.
- **Location and Access** - After students determine their priorities for information seeking, they must locate information from a variety of resources, access specific information found within individual resources, and evaluate the quality of resources.
- **Use of Information** - After finding potentially useful resources, students must engage (read, view, listen) the information to determine its relevance and then extract the relevant information.
- **Synthesis** - Students must organize and communicate the results of the information problem-solving effort.
- **Evaluation** - Evaluation focuses on how well the product meets the original task (effectiveness) and the process of how well students carried out the problem-solving process (efficiency). (e-Learning)

The plan described above is the Big6™ Approach to Information Problem Solving, perhaps the best known and most widely used approach to teaching information and technology skills. Also cited as an exemplary practice in the 21st Century Literacy Summit White Paper, the Big6 Skills (first developed in 1987) provides a systematic process based on six broad skill areas necessary for successful information problem solving. This approach builds a set of skills and an organized strategy for effectively meeting information needs while developing critical thinking skills.

1.6 Conclusion:

Currently, there is an emphasis on computers as tools - the use of word processing, presentation software (e.g., PowerPoint, HyperStudio), database systems, and electronic spreadsheets. But there is growing dissatisfaction with this piecemeal and often haphazard approach to technology in education. The great promise of technology to improve student performance remains unfulfilled. Increasingly, we see school boards, parents, and educators questioning the value, expense, and impact of technology in education.

We agree that the way technology has been implemented in schools should be questioned. We believe that the problems stem from the way technology has been introduced into education. Our vision - contemporary literacy - builds a bridge to connect current approaches to technology and traditional literacy. Contemporary literacy focuses on fundamental thinking and problem solving processes and describes how technology can be used within these processes to improve student achievement.

In this chapter, we have stressed that technology skills are only a first step in assuring all our children become proficient information and technology users. Similarly, contemporary literacy is more than just a laundry list of skills, literacies, and technologies. Chapter Two expands our vision of contemporary literacy by explaining how we can move from vision to practice.

1• Getting Started: Crafting a Shared Vision

"Schools are likely to be more successful in achieving in-depth learning when leaders work with staff and the community to build a collective educational vision that is clear, compelling, and connected to teaching and learning." Critical Issue: Building a Collective Vision <http://www.ncrel.org/sdrs/areas/ issues/ educatrs/leadrshp/le100.htm>

In *Information Technology for Learning* we have identified *contemporary literacy* as a critical component of our vision. Use the Big6 Matrix to familiarize your team members with the Big6 Skills and their relationship to contemporary literacy standards. <http://www.surfline.ne.jp/ janetm/big6info.htm>

Choose one activity from each of the six skills in the matrix to explore as a group. Guide your discussions with the following questions:

1 *Task Definition:* Can you use a graphic organizer to record the elements of your vision as you begin to discuss it?

2 *Information Seeking Strategies:* Which members of your school community must be involved in the process of establishing a vision?

3 *Location and Access:* How will you use technology to improve student achievement? What do you expect students to know and be able to do?

4 *Use of Information:* How will a shared understanding of contemporary literacy and national technology standards influence the goals and objectives you select?

5 *Synthesis:* Write a vision statement upon which all members of the committee and essential stakeholders can agree. Publish it widely; perhaps create a school motto or logo incorporating it.

6 *Evaluation:* Periodically re-examine your vision: does it clearly relate to the plans and strategies you have adopted? Is it helping teachers and parents stay focused on improving student achievement?

"The vision must include student learning. Emphasize higher-order thinking, problem solving, and other features of high-achieving learning environments to keep staff attention focused on student learning."

See also "Critical Issue: Building a Collective Vision" <http://www.ncrel.org/sdrs/ areas/issues/educatrs/leadrshp/le100.htm> for more guidance on building a collective vision.

chapter 2

Leading from Vision to Practice

We have a vision: contemporary literacy for all teachers and students will improve student achievement and promote lifelong learning that exceeds the accountability provisions of *No Child Left Behind* legislation. Schools are more than bricks and mortar: their design must be inspired with a view to what will be created and nurtured inside. Extending the construction analogy, the Big6 Skills provides the scaffolding from which we can assemble the answers to our information needs as we begin to remodel our school.

2.1 From Promise to Practice: The Big6™ Skills

Which models can guide us in moving from promise to practice?

"A number of authors have attempted to delineate the research process by creating broadly applicable models that describe a sequence of activities. The first three national information literacy standards, with their correlated indicators, reflect a synthesis of the research models that emphasizes the importance of information expertise in everyday life. (Information Power, p. 8) If the goal of schools is to create independent lifelong learners, they must integrate information literacy skills throughout the curriculum." (Murray, Information TeAchnology) Mike Eisenberg and associates compared a number of information skills process models (Eisenberg, Teaching, p. 17); examining their chart, it seems that all these models share common traits:

- Information literacy is viewed as the attainment of information skills within a process.
- Information literacy is central to and essential for student achievement in all curriculum and performance contexts.
- Information skills learning must take place in full integration with classroom curriculum and assignments.

The crucial importance of information literacy heightens the value of successful implementations. Lowe reports "Eisenberg and Berkowitz (1988) found that the best way to teach information literacy skills (such as the Big6) in curriculum context is through the collaboration of classroom teachers and library media specialists. Brievik (1998) found that the same is true in higher education, as students succeed in integrated courses designed by faculty members and academic librarians."(Lowe)

According to Eisenberg and Berkowitz (1990), the Big6 is an approach that can be used whenever people are faced with an information problem or with making a decision that is based on information. Students K-12 through higher education encounter many information problems related to course assignments. They must locate assigned readings, evaluate information

The Big6™ Skills

1. Task Definition
1.1 Define the information problem
1.2 Identify information needed in order to complete the task (to solve the information problem)

2. Information Seeking Strategies
2.1 Determine the range of possible sources (brainstorm)
2.2 Evaluate the different possible sources to determine priorities (select the best sources)

3. Location and Access
3.1 Locate sources (intellectually and physically)
3.2 Find information within sources

4. Use of Information
4.1 Engage (e.g., read, hear, view, touch) the information in a source
4.2 Extract relevant information from a source

5. Synthesis
5.1 Organize information from multiple sources
5.2 Present the information

6. Evaluation
6.1 Judge the product (effectiveness)
6.2 Judge the information problem-solving process (efficiency)

Big6™ Skills. Copyright ©1987. Eisenberg, M.B. & Berkowitz, R.E.

sources, and extract and compile information to write research papers. However, the Big6 model is just as applicable to their personal lives.

The Big6 Skills comprise a unified set of information and technology skills (see Sidebar). Taken together, these skills form a process. By using the Big6, people learn how to recognize their information needs and how to progress through a series of stages to solve information problems effectively and efficiently. Many problem-solving models provide a set of specific activities, or outline of isolated skills. However, "although they are useful to organize teachers' and students' thinking about research, the biggest failing of research models is that they describe a recursive process in linear terms. I tell students that 'research' literally means 'to search and search again.'" (Murray, Information TeAchnology)

Like these others, the Big6 approach is systematic; however, it differs in a significant way. The Big6 Skills provides a broad-based, logical skill set that can be used as the structure for developing a curriculum or the framework for a set of distinct problem-solving skills. But the Big6 is more than simply a set of skills - it is also an approach to helping students learn the information problem-solving process. Learning more about the Big6 as a process and as an approach should make it easier and more useful for teachers and their students. For teachers, the Big6 provides a definitive set of skills that students must master in order to be successful in any learning context. Teachers can integrate lessons about the Big6 into subject area content and assignments. For students, the Big6 provides a guide to dealing with assignments and tasks as well as a model to fall back on when they are stuck. The Big6 encourages "metacognition" - students' awareness of their mental states and processes.

I&T Team Snapshot from Timber Drive

In 1989, Nancy Finger (Library Media Specialist) was excited by the first articles about Flexible Access in *School Library Journal*. By 1992, she had attended every conference she could to learn more about putting the concepts into practice. In 1993-94, Wake County was one of several districts in the nation to be awarded a Library Power grant, which opened doors to the best thinkers and doers in the information literacy world. Through these doors came Mike Eisenberg, who introduced the Big6™ Skills to the district in 1997.

2.2 From Vision to Strategy: The Information & Technology Team
2.2.1 Leadership Through Teamwork

How can we provide the experiences necessary for students, educators, administrators and the community to master these contemporary literacy skills?

The harsh reality of Vermont winters has bred self-reliance over generations into a locally convincing worldview. Getting to "theyah" from "heyah" often requires building a bridge, which in turn, requires a team of people, supported by community resources and a well engineered plan. The less harsh but often as isolated reality of school classrooms has led to brilliant examples of self-reliant technology excellence, but until we take the team approach to bridge building, the Vermont farmer's advice rings all too true.

School districts encounter similar advice once they seek directions that will lead them to improved student achievement. "You can't get theyah from heyah" until you bridge potentials with practice, and design roads that reach all the way to your destinations. Two decades down the path of promises, the benefits of educational technology seem to reside in the eye of the beholder.

Those who have focused on purposes see more improved practice than those who have simply been dazzled by potentials.

It isn't a question of roadmaps or signs; it's a matter of realities - how you build the bridges and roads themselves. Here are four insights about leadership that have led me to believe in the power of teams:

- In any setting, people sense the presence (or absence) of leadership, and react accordingly.
- Leadership is based on permissions. These permissions are two-way, and require relationships, both for their creation and to be maintained.
- Relationships may begin individually, but are soon organized into groups. Groups, rather than individuals, form communities. Paradoxically, the effectiveness of groups is determined by the presence of passionate, dedicated individuals who've taken ownership of the message.
- As groups become more adept at communications, their actions are more likely to result in effective collaborations that meet the needs of communities. Conversely, until groups become capable communicators, sustained collaboration is impossible.

Whether you see technology as a promise or a challenge (or both) depends on your experience and your imagination. Over the past two decades, we've seen a parade of increasingly powerful experimental applications of technology for learning, yet far too often these lessons have yet to be integrated into daily life in every classroom. Only those who have personally experienced the power of 21st Century Learning can take the next step of imagining how to make it possible in every classroom, in every school.

We are finding ways to harness people's creativity and productivity all over the planet, and finally the time has come to begin doing this in our schools. It has always made sense to do so, but until now it hasn't seemed practical. With the advent of affordable, network capable computers, and the similar increase in power and decrease in cost of networking equipment, we can effectively argue that it is impractical to procrastinate bringing these new ways of working into one of the most important social functions we perform: the education of our citizens.

Let's be honest: the challenges are formidable. Scarce resources, scarcer technical expertise, and the ultimate scarcity of time conspire to put many of us into mañana mode. But we aren't talking about tomorrow, we're talking about what's being done today. There are schools that have created the time to find out how to gather the required expertise, and how to garner the support of their communities in order to provide the resources that build a foundation for their students' futures right now. The real key, no matter where you start from, is "we can't get there alone." That shift in perspective, from progress being seen as the aggregate of individual efforts, to the focused, sustained application of vision to strategy to implementation by the I&T Team, is what this book is all about.

Inspired by Mike Eisenberg and Carrie Lowe's article "Call to Action: Getting Serious about Libraries and Information in Education," we advocate the formation of **Information & Technology (I&T) Teams** at the building level, in order to provide the capacity for sustained support of educational improvement. The members of the I&T Team are the people in schools who are most involved in the implementation of technology: the principal, the library media specialist, the teacher leader (defined by Margaret Riel and Hank Becker as "teachers who place a high value on sharing their knowledge with their teaching colleagues") and the technical specialist (supported by the District Technology Coordinator). Note, we don't say support for *technology*: the efforts must remain firmly fixed on the goal of system wide improvement at the school level, with the role of technology clearly as servant rather than master.

The following excerpts provide an introduction to the I&T Team concept. Chapter Three describes the members of the I&T Team, and Chapter Four describes what they must do, in order to achieve the vision of contemporary literacy for all learners.

2.2.2 Excerpt from "Call to Action: Getting Serious about Libraries and Information in Education" by Michael B. Eisenberg and Carrie Lowe

Schools with strong, committed Information & Technology Teams invariably see great results in their schools, and not only in terms of what their students are learning. These collaborative programs enjoy excellent funding, the respect of their colleagues, and influence over administrative decisions.

The members of the Information & Technology Team can be found within your own school: technology teachers, library and information professionals, and key administrators. All you need to add is commitment, enthusiasm, and teamwork. A unified I&T Team is one where team members work together to provide services and resources to classroom teachers, students, and even parents.

The work of the Information & Technology Team goes beyond creating a technology-rich learning environment for students, although this is one of their most important tasks. Great I&T Teams have a close relationship with classroom teachers and administration, and their responsibilities affect every aspect of the school. They provide a technical support system by coordinating tech services and resources and coordinating purchasing decisions. In terms of curriculum, the I&T Team oversees the information and technology literacy program and ensures that it is implemented as part of the classroom curriculum. An active, dynamic Information & Technology Team is an integral part of the school; they are the right arm of overburdened administrators and teachers.

Unfortunately, at this time, we don't see enough of these I&T Teams in schools and districts. Too often we see library media specialists, technology teachers, and administrators working in isolation and fighting for turf and control. At the same time, these educators bemoan their feelings of professional disenfranchisement, their inability to interest colleagues in collaboration, being overwhelmed with just too much to do, and worst of all, budget cuts and eliminated positions. Although they all say that they are working toward a common goal - preparing students for success in the information age - they are not working together.

It is possible for library media specialists and technology teachers to work together with administrators and other educators. It is not simply possible; it is necessary that they do so in order to become the active players in curriculum and instruction that they must be in the coming decades to ensure the success of students in the information age.

Can library media specialists, technology teachers, and classroom teachers be replaced by technology? Absolutely not. We believe just the opposite. Library and information technology professionals are the true innovators of using technology to facilitate learning. As technology becomes more prevalent in learning and teaching, there is even greater need for information, library, and technology work in schools. This is a role that librarians can and must assume to create information-literate students. (19-20)

2.2.3 Timber Drive Elementary School

What distinguishes Timber Drive Elementary School in Garner, North Carolina from most other schools is the way in which collaborative planning and teaching embrace technology to reach every child. Throughout Chapter Four, you'll get a feel for how this team makes learning come alive for everyone in its community.

Timber Drive is a year-round school in which the traditional 180-day school year is divided into nine-week quarters with a three-week break at the end of each quarter. Students are in school the same number of days as their counterparts in traditional schools; their days are simply redistributed throughout the year. The reorganized schedule is called a 45/15 calendar - 45 days in school, 15 days off.

When Principal Sue King opened Timber Drive Elementary School in 1997, she left nothing to chance. She developed a leadership team that applied the many lessons learned in their previous schools, making collaboration, trust and teambuilding a part of Timber Drive's DNA before the doors even opened, before any teacher was hired.

Having an I&T Team that knows it is a team and embraces its role for school wide improvement is rare. An elementary school with two full time

Library Media Specialists and a Network Administrator is unheard of. How did this happen?

"It is so rewarding for us as administrators, because we know it works. When we're in budget planning time at the school, we get to decide how we will add to our staff (when enrollment goes up, we are allocated more personnel). Our leadership team, supported unanimously by our 55-60 teachers, has added three key positions over the years (two full time Library Media Specialists, a media assistant and one full time Network Administrator) beyond those that the state will provide us. This shows that the staff understands the vital contribution to the educational well being of the entire school, as a learning community, that our I&T team makes," notes Mrs. King.

"Far too often, there is an emphasis on how to use (operate) computers, but not enough people are reaching for the next level: how do I integrate technology as a tool for instruction and learning?" That is the level Timber Drive strives for, and more schools should aspire to.

What benefits can schools with strong, committed Information & Technology Teams expect? The members of great I&T Teams work together to create technology-rich learning environments that feature computers and computer applications as essential tools for improved achievement.

2.3 Strong Medicine: Scientifically Based Research, School Practice and Accountability

How can the I&T Team model help us address the accountability requirements of No Child Left Behind?

The passage of the ESEA *No Child Left Behind* Act (NCLB) profoundly alters the education landscape by shifting the focus away from "inputs" and onto student results. *No Child Left Behind* fundamentally changes how education is paid for, and how technology fits into the process. The profound, yet subtle shift from researching "does technology work?" to "what are the

2• Getting Started: How to Build Your I&T Team

"Effective team functioning requires finding time, selecting team members, empowering team members, providing training in relevant skills and knowledge, developing shared goals, and facilitating team functioning - particularly in the early stages of the team's work." Critical Issue: Building a Committed Team <http://www.ncrel.org/sdrs/areas/issues/educatrs/leadrshp/le200.htm>

1 Identify the prospective members of your team:
      Building Administrator: _____
      Teacher Leader: _____
      Library Media Specialist: _____
      Technical Specialist: _____
      District Technology Coordinator: _____

2 Do they already work well together as a team? Or will this be a new experience? [Consider possible barriers to effective teamwork: Do they already know each other but have a history of personal and/or professional interactions that may interfere with their ability to work as a team? Do one or more of them resist "playing games"?] Depending on your assessment, choose one or more of the following teambuilding activities:

    A   Get Acquainted: Human Scavenger Hunt <http://www.gamesfor groups.com/mixitup.htm>
    B   Work as a Team: Bridge Toss <http://www.gamesforgroups.com/teamup.htm>
    C   Activity of the Month: Check the free teambuilding activities at http:// www.learningunlimited.com/Activityofmonth/index.asp

3 Explicitly address the need for team norms and expectations for effective communication. Print copies of the description of effective teams at http://www. nsba.org/sbot/toolkit/LeadTeams.html to guide your discussion. See also "Critical Issue: Building a Committed Team" <http://www.ncrel.org/sdrs/areas/issues/educatrs/leadrshp/le200.htm> for more guidance on building an effective team.

conditions under which technology improves student learning?" opens an enormous opportunity for all educators.

In passing *No Child Left Behind*, Congress has mandated that funding decisions and practice should adhere to **Scientifically Based Research (SBR)**. NCLB's accountability provisions require that states set annual performance goals for schools, based on the percentage of students scoring at a proficient level on state reading and math assessments.

In native American cultures, medicine evokes dimensions of power that go beyond the clinical aspects of the western medical model. In this sense, SBR is strong medicine for the education community, providing powerful motivations to shift to instructional practice informed by scientifically based research.

Double-Click: Threat or Promise?

The new technology represents the greatest threat to organized education ever... Why do I say that technology is a threat? Because it creates the opportunity for cheating -widespread dishonesty in an unparalleled way.

The other major threat comes from the values driving technology; that is, if technology is used to make schooling more efficient and cheaper, then we're going to drive people away from learning. If technology is harnessed to try to produce a single measure of learning that is both reliable and valid, we'll end up with even more machine-scored exams, and we'll narrow the curriculum to teach only that which can easily be tested. (Merrow)

We are not mere passengers; we are the drivers for the journey into evidence-based practice. The I&T Team plays a critical role in identifying the needs that will shape the prioritization of research. The I&T Team's efforts to share and replicate evidence-based interventions will do more to "build a culture of scientific inquiry" within our profession than could ever be achieved through mere legislation.

2.3.1 Balancing Accountability, Achievement and Growth

It's simple. Or is it? For the next twelve years, these performance goals must rise in equal increments, until all students are proficient in reading and math. In addition, each student subgroup (e.g., race, income, gender, English proficiency) must meet the same annual performance goals. When schools have met these expectations (for each subgroup) they have met their **Adequate Yearly Progress (AYP)** goals.

Of course, the devil is in the details. The accountability provisions of *No Child Left Behind* confront schools with unprecedented challenges, played out in 50 states in 50 ways. Each state decides what constitutes **adequate yearly progress**, based upon student performance on its statewide assessments. Student data is disaggregated so that lack of performance by one subgroup isn't offset by performance gains from another. Schools are the unit of measure, either meeting or failing to meet AYP goals. *No Child Left Behind* specifies five levels of consequences for each year schools fail to meet AYP goals, from withholding funds to taking over the school.

For some, the anticipated results may be difficult to face. "For the first time, we're telling the truth about all of our kids, and that's the only thing that has changed. Before, we ignored student failure, but now we're being honest and confronting student failure. Everybody has to be able to look at the statistics, and when they look at the statistics, the inevitable conclusion is that we must do something about student achievement, particularly in our lowest-income and minority populations," according to Lisa Graham Keegan, Director of the Education Leaders' Council.

We are at a pivotal moment regarding education and society, a moment that challenges us to focus information and technology skills on the process of improving education. For once, the course of action we advocate aligns with the general public's high priorities for (and deep concerns about) the direction and quality of learning provided by the public education system. When our actions are understood as a concerted

The Role of Technology in Accountability

"The accountability sections of [the Elementary and Secondary Education Act] will not only require schools to perform better instructionally, but to document how and to what extent they are doing so," said Raymond Yeagley, superintendent of the Rochester, N.H., Public Schools.

"Data-driven decision making has been the norm in the sciences for more than a century," Yeagley continued. "You wouldn't want a surgeon selecting a particular procedure for your illness because he or she had heard that a hospital down the road had a couple of success stories." But that's exactly how schools make many of their decisions now, he said.

"To generate these data ... the district will have to rely on technology and, more importantly, will need to have someone on staff with enough technical knowledge to extract the data from their original sources, convert them to a format readable by the analysis tool, and assure that they don't become contaminated in the conversion process," he said.

Yeagley said he believes the new accountability requirements will demand that schools subject their data to at least a rudimentary statistical analysis, and "that can't be done effectively without technology." (eSN)

effort to improve school and student performance, we can tap in to powerful community impulses to join and support this effort.

3• Getting Started: Taking Stock of Available Resources and Needs

1 Direct each member of your team to fill out NCREL's "Learning with Technology Profile Tool" <http://www.ncrtec.org/capacity/profile/profile.htm> Compare your results. Do your individual assessments tend to agree? If not, examine and discuss the disparities.

2 Assess the needs of your students. Use the Quality School Portfolio's Data Manager <http://qsp.cse.ucla.edu/> to disaggregate and analyze data from standardized tests. On which skills do your students need more help?

3 Compile the results of your assessments in graphs that will be easy for all teachers to understand. Share them with the entire faculty as well as community members.

2.3.2 Baldrige Education Criteria for Performance Excellence

We are guided by a vision for engaging "students in the learning process in order to help them attain the higher standards set for today's learners and tomorrow's leaders," a vision we share with the Baldrige *Education Criteria for Performance Excellence.*

The Malcolm Baldrige Education Criteria provide the basis for assessment and feedback to organizations and create the foundation for an organization's continuous improvement journey. The criteria have three important purposes:

1 To help improve performance practices, capabilities, and results;
2 To facilitate communication and sharing of best practices information among organizations of all types;
3 To serve as a working tool for understanding and improving performance and for guiding planning and opportunities for learning.

The Baldrige Criteria for Performance Excellence provide a systems perspective for understanding performance management. They reflect validated, leading-edge management practices against which an organization can measure itself. With their acceptance nationally and internationally as the model for performance excellence, the criteria represent a common language for communication among organizations for sharing best practices. The criteria are also the basis for the Baldrige National Quality Award process.

The I&T Team will need to take a leadership role in managing data and turning it into knowledge for improved performance. Key areas of the Baldrige process that focus these skills on education improvement are information and analysis, faculty/staff focus, process management and results. (See Sidebar "Baldrige Core Values and Concepts")

2.4 Flying Blind? 21st Century Navigation Tools for Improved Learning

Maps tell you where things are in relation to one another, but won't tell you where you are. A compass tells you which way you are headed, but not your speed or altitude.

Baldrige Core Values and Concepts

The Baldrige Core Values and Concepts are embodied in seven categories:

1 **LEADERSHIP** - to be effective, leaders must understand the Baldrige model and core values and communicate to the workforce and leadership system their intention to use that model for assessment and improvement. Leaders need to understand the system and realize that it is their responsibility to share the knowledge and set direction.

2 **STRATEGIC PLANNING** - critical to this category is that every person in the organization must know the strategic plan and be able to describe how he or she contributes to achieving the plan's goals and objectives.

3 **STUDENT/STAKEHOLDER FOCUS** - engaging students in the educational planning and decisions that affect them will have the largest payback in terms of performance and a positive organizational climate.

4 **INFORMATION AND ANALYSIS** - key goals need to be measurable in clear and understandable ways. In the best organizations and classrooms, information is used to drive actions. Mature, high-performing organizations collect data on competitors and similar providers and compare themselves against world-class leaders.

5 **FACULTY/STAFF FOCUS** - faculty and staff are viewed as the most valuable asset of the organization and investment and development are critical to achieving the organization's mission and goals.

6 **PROCESS MANAGEMENT** - key to improving organizational performance is the ability to identify key processes and manage them so that student and stakeholder requirements are met consistently.

7 **RESULTS** - the proof that what an organization identifies as important is being accomplished and success overtime is evident. (Adapted from Mark Blazey, author of Insights to Performance Excellence in Education.)

(Baldrige)

Radar pinpoints your location, but unless someone tracks your progress, your safe arrival is left to chance. Aviation knows that only a system with the proper tools and effective procedures that are understood by all parties within a distributed team can safely convey everyone from departure to destination.

By contrast, education's over-reliance on mandated high-stakes testing for accountability (instead of a coordinated, multi-faceted system designed to guide growth) may lead to undesired outcomes. Unless and until critical

The Organizational Profile:
A Starting Point for Self-Assessment

The following material is excerpted from *Education Criteria for Performance Excellence.*

The Organizational Profile is a snapshot of your organization: the key influences on how you operate and the key challenges you face. The first section, Organizational Description, addresses your organization's educational environment and your key relationships with students, stakeholders, suppliers, and other partners. The second section, Organizational Challenges, calls for a description of your organization's competitive environment, your key strategic challenges, and your system for performance improvement. If you identify topics for which conflicting, little, or no information is available, it is possible that your assessment need go no further and you can use these topics for action planning.

Organizations depend on the measurement and analysis of performance. Such measurements should derive from the organization's needs and strategy, and they should provide critical data and information about key processes and results. Many types of data and information are needed for performance management. Performance measurement should focus on student learning, which requires a comprehensive and integrated fact-based system - one that includes input data, environmental data, performance data, comparative/competitive data, data on faculty and staff, cost data, and operational performance measurement.

Measurement areas might include students' backgrounds, learning styles, aspirations, academic strengths and weaknesses, educational progress, classroom and program learning, satisfaction with instruction and services, extracurricular activities, dropout/matriculation rates, and postgraduation success.

Analysis refers to extracting larger meaning from data and information to support evaluation, decision making, and operational improvement. Analysis entails using data to determine trends, projections, and cause and effect that might not otherwise be evident. Analysis supports a variety of purposes, such as planning, reviewing your overall performance, improving operations, change management, and comparing your performance with comparable organizations or with "best practices" benchmarks.

A major consideration in performance improvement and change management involves the selection and use of performance measures or indicators. The measures or indicators you select should best represent the factors that lead to improved student, operational, and financial performance. A comprehensive set of measures or indicators tied to student, stakeholder, and/or organizational performance requirements represents a clear basis for aligning all activities with your organization's goals. Through the analysis of data from your tracking processes, your measures or indicators themselves may be evaluated and changed to better support your goals.

information is collected, interpreted, and communicated between responsible parties in a timely way, neither flight nor learning can work on a mass scale.

What are the maps, compasses, radar, and safety systems for 21st century learning? Which technology-based tools are available to construct systems to guide learning much as air traffic control guides flights? Which resources can guide your path to 21st century learning so that no child, teacher, class or school fails to meet desired expectations?

2.4.1 Learning Management Systems: Key Elements

The foundational concept for **Learning Management Systems (LMS)** is making the right data available, to the people who need it, by their preferred method, at the right time. The needs of different users reflect their different purposes, the ways they use the data, and the environments in which they work. Computers are not the only way people interact with information. Some parents might need access by phone, or in print. Administrators might need access from anywhere in the school district. Teachers might need access from their classroom as well as home. The network must be designed to support each user and their needs, in order to remove barriers to their participation and contributions.

No matter what you call them, no matter which combination of capabilities they offer, there are four key elements that a successful **learning management system** provides:

- Instruction,
- Assessment,
- Communication,
- Professional Development.

Did students learn the targeted standards? Who did this lesson reach; do I need to rethink it? Do students remember what they studied last semester? Are some students ready to move on to the next lesson? Do some kids meet their learning goals more consistently when they share their progress with the rest of the class? What strategies have other teachers successfully used to meet similar challenges of students we're having trouble reaching now? Each of these questions touches all four aspects that must be addressed by a comprehensive learning management system.

It becomes complex when the other aspects of the "education enterprise" are linked to the system, to provide data to inform decisions about how investments of time, money and talent are contributing to the bottom line of enhanced student performance. These include:

- student information system,
- business office enterprise system (accounting/purchasing, payroll, Human Resources),
- transportation system,
- food service system,
- library automation system,
- student health software,
- special education management software, and
- curriculum management software.

Guess who gets to make it work? That's right: a team! The technical aspects of providing sufficiently reliable, accessible infrastructure to support the "mission critical" applications that comprise a learning management system are among the responsibilities of the district technology coordinator, the Principal and the building technical specialist.

2.4.2 My Father's Boat

While researching this section, I interviewed Jim McVety, Senior Analyst with Eduventures, Inc., concerning the "state of the art" in data-driven decision making. He offered the following analogy: for many years, his family enjoyed his father's 24-foot fishing boat. However, there was one seemingly simple question whose complex answer provides a great metaphor for anyone seeking to implement a learning management system: "how old is your boat?"

On the surface, the boat had been purchased at a certain point in time, but by the time the question was raised, apart from the steering wheel and the hull, just about everything else had been replaced. The engines, the navigation system, the radio, the decks, the bunks, the galley...there was never enough money to buy an entire new boat, so pieces were replaced as they broke, or upgraded as needed. The components that went to sea in that original hull had dozens of birth dates, making the question impossible to answer with a single age.

Schools will most likely find themselves in a similar predicament. Faced with the choice of buying a new yacht, or the pieces, they will find that the cost of scrapping everything they have is too high. They may have recently replaced their library automation system, desire a new student information system, and be limping along on a payroll system that still works, but not so well.

Jim's advice to schools is two-fold:

- Inventory - determine what you've got, and what it will work with;
- Data-Warehouse - capture and mine the information required to make evidence-based operational decisions.

In sailboat racing, the drag created by barnacles, or a line trailing over the side, can slow you down by hundredths of seconds, enough to determine the outcome. Every possible source of drag is considered, checked for, and eliminated. Yet in schools, we sometimes drag anchor, by perpetuating practices that no longer make any contribution to student learning. The goal of administrators is to redirect resources in ways that free up the time, money and talent desperately needed to improve student performance. Some schools have paid for their entire networking infrastructure simply by changing their phone system; for example, Princeton (N.J.) Regional Schools put in fiber between buildings, changed their switchboard and eliminated local phone charges. Learning management systems put in place procedures that gather all pertinent information regarding performance of all parts of the system, and provide analysis that informs decision-makers about how they can do more with less.

No matter what system you implement, professional development is the key. Such professional development needs to address questions like these:

Inventory of Current Practices

- How do we grow the abilities of teachers and students to harness these systems to guide their next steps in learning and teaching?
- How do we learn to see patterns that can inform our choices about curriculum and instruction?
- What information do we currently track? How do we use it to improve?
- How do we determine when and how to analyze and share the data with our teachers so they can use it to improve?

4• Getting Started: Charting Your Journey

1 Use NCREL's "Trip Planner Survey Tool" <http://www.ncrel.org/sdrs/trip/welcome.htm> to identify and prioritize your school's needs.

2 Develop a school improvement plan based on your assessments (including those in Worksheet 3). Use the resources at NCREL's "Pathways to School Improvement" site: <http://www.ncrel.org/sdrs/>

3 Identify a schoolwide intervention and apply it systematically. Consider locally administered assessments that will fit your needs; see the Resource Kit at Quality School Portfolio: <http://qsp.cse.ucla.edu/> Develop pre and post-tests to assess the effects of your chosen interventions.

2.4.3 Evaluating Your Evaluation

Do you trust your instruments? How do you know if they're working? Having a gas gauge that is stuck on "Full" is no better than having one that's stuck on "Empty." You also must plan a process that checks whether or not your assessment and evaluation methods are providing reliable data. This is why it's crucial to use multiple measures, and to triangulate the results across these measures, to see whether they provide information that is valid.

2.5 Conclusion: I&T Teams with a Vision and a Mission

The skills and capabilities required for success in the 21st Century are embedded in the tools and tasks that comprise the I&T team's daily work. Although the elements for success exist in your school, they lie dormant until they are aligned to support the compelling vision of contemporary literacy in the digital age. We see what must be done, but the job is too big for any one of us. That's why we advocate forming teams at the building level, bringing together the expertise of diverse professionals to focus their efforts in a coordinated way. Not only do we intuitively know that such a course of action is right, we are riding a wave of change that traverses all elements of society. For once, the communities who provide context for our work in schools seem to understand the imperative that schools prepare our children for the challenges and responsibilities that become theirs when they leave our care. In order to leave no school behind, there are specific strategies and resources you can apply to your situation. The remainder of this book is dedicated to helping you succeed at this task.

chapter 3

Leadership Roles:

**Which Hats
Do You Wear?**

3.1 Overview

"Systems thinking is understanding the connections between people and processes in organizations. Performance of the system depends on how the parts fit, not on how good the parts are." (Preuss "One Page") Our systems approach leads to our fundamental assumption that the formation of **Information & Technology Teams**, comprised of the people who play key roles at the building level (principal, school library media specialist, teacher leader and technical specialist) is the best strategy for surviving the challenges of educational technology.

Most schools don't have onsite support for technology. Many have neither full time library media specialists nor teacher leaders who've been given the time and resources to help their peers apply technology effectively in their classrooms. Most building level principals have too many other responsibilities to have learned to be effective technology users themselves.

Information Technology for Learning takes a systems approach to enhancing learning. Systems thinking shares with literacy a prematurely positive reaction from most people, before they agree about what it means. Accordingly, before we begin discussing the roles that are played by the I&T Team, it is important that we share a foundation of understandings about how systems thinking plays out in schools. Dr. Paul Preuss, assistant superintendent for Instruction and Planning at the Herkimer Board of Cooperative Educational Services (BOCES) located in central New York State, shared his thoughts in this "One Page Systems Primer," which can provide us with a firm foundation from which to examine the challenges and our responses.

3.1.1 "A One Page Systems Primer"

Understanding and application of "systems thinking" is so fundamental to our ability to improve organizational outcomes that to function without them is not only a waste of time and resources but a fraud to all those involved.

There is so much more about systems than can be placed on a single page - however, the information below should be helpful in getting you started down the systems path and in providing insights into concepts underlying unified planning.

- Most problems are caused by the system - not people. Management controls the system. Therefore, management "owns" the problem.
- Organizational charts do not describe your system - flow charts do.
- Leaders must learn to understand and manage systems as opposed to individual, isolated events.

- Improving one part of a system without improving others may make things worse. If you focus on optimization of parts you will not improve the system.
- Systems nest within systems (leaf-tree-forest) (district-school-class)
- Systems resist change.
- Systems thinking is understanding the connections between people and processes in organizations. Performance of the system depends on how the parts fit, not on how good the parts are.
- Systems thinking is learning to see the whole. When a system is taken apart it loses its essential properties.
- Systems thinkers believe that structure influences behavior.
- Systems are not the sum of their parts - they are the product of their interactions.
- All long-term objectives can best be met by improving the processes that make up the system.
- The leader's primary role is to help people and processes do a better job.
- The people who work in a process are usually the best source of ideas and suggestions for improving that process.
- People naturally want to contribute, to do a good job, and to experience joy and pride in the work they do.
- Students naturally want to learn, to do a good job, and to experience pride and joy in learning.

With homage to: Dr. Russell Ackoff, Dr. W. Edwards Deming, Jimmy Chancey, Gelareh Asayesh, Jim Leonard, Dr. Peter Senge and many others from whom I have learned about systems. (Preuss "One Page")

The overview of the I&T Team's roles, *Defining the Roles*, should be read by everyone, in order to understand the talents and experience the person playing each role brings to your team. The subsequent sections, *Wearing the Hats*, should be consulted whenever you need more detail and guidance about playing any particular role.

3.1.2 Defining the Wizard's Role: Managing Systems (District Level - Chief Technology Officer (CTO) or Tech/Curriculum Coordinator)

Definition: Wizard - the person who knows about managing systems and processes for technology at the district level.

Is there a difference between magic and miracle? Although Arthur Clarke tells us "any sufficiently advanced technology is indistinguishable from magic," more often it seems it will take miracles to provide the reliable services educators must have, if they are to improve learning through the use of technology. We see magic as tricks or illusions that let our minds believe we've just witnessed something that can't be possible. Miracles, on the other hand, imply divine intervention, superseding the laws of nature.

The wizardry required of the **District Technology Coordinator** depends on the laws of nature, both physical and human. We are not speaking here about raising student achievement through levitation. It takes hard, sustained, coordinated work. Instead, our alchemy depends on blending individual talents into teams.

The incredible growth of the Internet and Intranet infrastructure in education has created a need for district leadership:

- helping administrators and classroom teachers to meet new competencies;
- setting new priorities and re-evaluating past teaching practices in order to make use of the latest technologies;
- coordinating overall technology planning, hardware/software acquisition, implementation, budget oversight and grant writing, teacher professional development, maintenance and upgrades, and curriculum support.

Anyone who's ready to take on that set of challenges deserves to wear the wizard's hat!

3.1.3 Defining The Pilot's Role: Managing People (Building Level - Principal)

Definition: Pilot - the person who knows about managing people, schedules and budgets at the building level.

In the days of the barnstormers, the pilot was often the only passenger. Particularly brave (or foolhardy, depending on your point of view) individuals would sometimes go up for a ride, returning to earth with stories they could tell their children and grandchildren. But now, air travel has become routine. The pilot no longer flies the plane: computers do. The complexity of systems required to keep a modern jetliner aloft extend far beyond the capabilities of any individual. Like technology in schools, it is a team effort.

However, we still need pilots. Someone must take responsibility for knowing our destination and monitoring conditions in order to respond to changing circumstances in a manner that will allow us all to arrive safely. Unlike aircraft, schools have no *autopilot* upon which to rely; there is no substitute for the leadership that only the principal can provide at the building level.

The pilot monitors fuel, direction, progress on the flight plan, as well as modifications that may be required en route. There are plans to address a range of potential onboard emergencies, and the pilot monitors the crew in terms of their readiness to address any that may arise.

This analogy can't go the distance, however. Pilots receive extensive training about the capabilities and requirements of the systems they manage. Principals don't enjoy similar preparation to lead technology-rich environments. Their preparation reverts back to the bailing-wire and bubblegum fixes of the barnstorming era, if they are willing to go aloft at all. What can the principal rely upon for guidance?

3.1.4 Defining the Scholar's Role: Managing Knowledge (Library Media Specialist)

Definition: Scholar - the person who knows about locating information and organizing knowledge.

Librarians learn the skills of scholarship and the art of information retrieval in graduate programs in library and information science. Although it is not widely known outside their ranks, school library media specialists (LMS) hold dual citizenship in the worlds of teaching and information science. In schools with effective technology programs, one often finds the LMS and the media center at the core, with effective partnerships reaching out to all classrooms. Managing knowledge is quite different from managing learning, and requires different interactions with people, resources and activities. This is one reason why the partnerships that comprise effective I&T teams can be so powerful. Understanding the role of the library media specialist is crucial to developing such an effective team.

3.1.5 Defining the Guide's Role: Managing Learners (Teacher Leader)

Definition: Guide - the person who knows about designing and implementing learning experiences, and has the most daily contact with a particular set of children.

In *The Beliefs, Practices, and Computer Use of Teacher Leaders*, Margaret Riel and Hank Becker define *teacher leaders* as "teachers who place a high value on sharing their knowledge with their teaching colleagues." (Riel) Teacher leaders are willing, and even eager, to examine their own practices and try new methods of instruction to improve their students' achievement. They tend to use collaborative learning and project-based learning more enthusiastically and effectively than their colleagues. They were early adopters of technology, and have integrated the use of computers with their classroom instruction. They have invested heavily in their own continuing education; they model the importance of lifelong learning in their classrooms and their professional interactions. Most important, they are willing to work collaboratively with their colleagues to design the most effective learning experiences for their students.

3.1.6 Defining the Hard Hat's Role: Managing Resources (Technical Specialist)

Definition: Hard Hat - the person who knows about making hardware, software and networks function.

This role is often confused with that of a firefighter, because the technical specialist is usually asked to drop whatever she or he is doing to put out some technical fire. In reality, the health of the infrastructure depends more on careful design and building, on taking the time to maintain what's there and to educate users about how to avoid creating problems. That's why we've chosen the "hard hat" as an image. The technical specialist applies the District's guidelines to the local building or school network, installing hardware and software, maintaining backups and firewalls, and trouble-shooting workstation and printer problems. The hard hat helps construct interactive workspaces on the network and helps teachers and administrators learn to use them effectively.

Finding the balance between what technology can do and the ability of people to utilize it presents the major challenge for this role: it is the people rather than the equipment that are most problematic. No wonder so many tech specialists seem to prefer fixing things that don't work to working with people who don't seem to be willing to learn. Bridging this gulf is one of the most important tasks for the I&T Team.

5• Getting Started: Potlatch - What Can You Offer?

The teamwork we advocate is similar to the Potlatch of the Northwest Native Americans, where the entire community gathered to assemble, celebrate and redistribute the riches that had been generated individually. In your school, ideas for insight and actions can replace material wealth as a medium of exchange.

1. Now that you have read the description of leadership roles for each of the members of your team, identify the "hats" you will wear, and describe the contributions you can make to the work of your team.

2. What are your unique skills?

3. What decisions do you control?

4. What evidence can you gather through your daily interactions with staff, students, parents?

5. Share your reflections with the members of your team. Assess the strengths of the individuals on your team and assign responsibilities for leadership in the following areas:

Task	Wizard	Pilot	Scholar	Guide	Hard Hat
crafting the vision					
developing the school improvement plan					
developing the technology plan					
designing effective interventions					
collecting and analyzing data					
designing professional development activities					

3.2 Wearing the Wizard's Hat: Managing Systems (District Level - Chief Technology Officer (CTO) or Tech/Curriculum Coordinator)
3.2.1 What Does the Job Entail?

The **wizard's** primary role is to provide leadership for and manage implementation of technology in instructional and managerial applications. This role generally includes the following responsibilities:

1 Chair the District Technology Council or Committee. In addition, serve as a member of each working curriculum committee. Provide technology articulation in the district. Evaluate the technology curriculum and how technology is infused into each curriculum.

2 Report to the school board and administration on a yearly basis as to the status of technology in the district.

3 Maintain an accurate inventory of technology equipment. Maintain an efficient system of cataloging technology equipment and materials.

4 Oversee implementation of the District Technology Plan. Direct annual technology needs assessment and long-range planning.

5 Research hardware and software options. Provide input on purchase of all hardware to technology committee and administration. Develop and coordinate a time line for additional hardware purchases with the superintendent. Review and evaluate new commercial software as it is developed and communicate such evaluation to the instructional leaders of the district.

6 Install hardware components. Install software and software updates. Monitor software use for copyright compliance. Implement security systems.

7 Serve as network administrator for all facility networks. Administer and support the networks on a day-to-day basis.

8 Provide professional development programs in technology. Assist teachers in technology activity development and execution.

9 Interface with the district maintenance department. Supervise the maintenance of all technology equipment in the PK-12 buildings and provide service if possible for minor repairs to the equipment and the networks.

10 Initiate grants and cooperative ventures. Initiate business and community cooperation.

11 Represent the district at area or state meetings that focus on computer technology and education.

3.2.2 What Does the Wizard's Job Look Like, Across the Nation?

In cooperation with the Michigan Center for Technology Coordinators sponsored by the College of Education at Western Michigan University, *School, Planning and Management Magazine*, in April 1998, mailed 1,100 surveys to school districts with more than 600 students addressed to the person primarily responsible for technology. (Bete)

According to the survey,

> More than 165 technology directors replied (a response rate of 14.3%) representing 1.9% of the 9,067 districts with more than 600 students. Large, medium and small districts were represented with 20% of respondents having 600 to 2,499 students; 31% having 2,500 to 4,999 students; 20% having 5,000 to 9,999 students; 21% having 10,000 to 24,999 students; and 8% having more than 25,000 students. Responses came from every region of the country. (Bete)

The survey dealt with job titles, the technology coordinator's location in the chain of command, responsibilities, experience and educational background, administration support, and the all-important salary. While some of the responses were expected, many were very surprising.

Who actually supervises technology will greatly affect its direction in your district. According to the survey, more than half of the technology directors/coordinators report directly to the superintendent. Depending upon the structure of the district and its stage in technology integration, another 20% report to either an assistant superintendent or curriculum supervisor. Surprisingly, perhaps since the position may require certain needs assessments as well as budget predictions, some report to the business officer.

Most school district powers that be do not fully understand the complexities of a networked campus; therefore they do not fully understand the scope of work involved. Rob Reilly poses the question, "How many people do we need if one is NOT enough?" (40) Citing real world sources, Reilly documents the fact that one person cannot possibly do all that is expected of them by the district. The minimum staff should be a team of three depending upon the size of the district.

The expectations of the district can also be seen in survey results indicating the level of support districts have given technology coordinators. The support can be in the form of an assigned staff, but it also comes in the amount of time the district allows the top technology person to do an effective job.

When asked what percentage of their assigned responsibilities were for technology, almost 10% responded that they spend less than half of their time on issues related to technology.

When asked about the level of staff support, a whopping 21% of respondents had no staff whatsoever. According to the results of the survey "An additional 17% have only one to three employees reporting to them. At the other end of the spectrum, 22% of respondents have ten or more staff reporting to them." (Bete)

State Endorsements in Technology Coordination

The following is a list of states and government entities that have a technology coordination endorsement and a web site where you may access the full text:

New Mexico: Information Technology Coordinator links to a pdf document. <http://sde.state.nm.us/divisions/ais/licensure/competencies/index.html>

Wisconsin: Instructional Technology Coordinator submitted to the DPI Teacher Licensing Office - April 4, 2000 <http://www.dpi.state.wi.us/dltcl/imt/tekcordlic.html>

Department of Defense Educational Activity: Educational Technologist has a very nice handbook. <http://www.odedodea.edu/edprogram/ETHandbook/ETHandbook.html>

Washington: A Technology Coordinator Homepage with lots of good links to information. <http://www.ac.wwu.edu/ ~kenr/TCsite/home.html>

Arkansas: School District Technology Coordinator Roles and Responsibilities <http://arkedu.state.ar.us/ ade-guide/tech_coord.html>

North Carolina: NC Technology Competencies for Educators - Advanced <http://www.ncpublicschools.org/ tap/advance.htm>

3.2.3 State Recommended Technology Coordinator Competencies

Exactly what role does the state play in providing a job description for those districts that are struggling with this issue? Most states have developed teacher competencies related to using technology tools. Some are written by the states themselves and some borrow heavily from the *National Educational Technology Standards for Teachers (NETS-T)*. Technology Standards for School Administrators were released in 2001 (TSSA). <see http://cnets.iste.org/docs/States_using_NETS.pdf> However, only a handful of states have developed competencies specifically for technology coordinators, since the position is so new and the responsibilities are so varied.

3.3 Wearing the Pilot's Hat: Managing People (Building Level - Principal)

In the analogy of the modern pilot, we can see that the pilot or principal each must depend upon the team. The synergy between specialists, once united by a shared vision, allow these strengths to contribute to completion of the journey.

Successful school improvement requires establishing a clear educational vision and a shared institutional mission, knowing how well the school is accomplishing that mission, identifying areas for improvement, developing plans to change educational activities and programs, and implementing those plans or new programs effectively. It is essential that leaders of school improvement link to others in the school and district and connect the school's goals to the broader and deeper mission of providing high-quality learning for all students. Leaders also must consider equity issues when developing and implementing change initiatives - asking themselves, for example, whether a proposed program will improve access to higher-order learning tasks for marginalized students.

For school improvement efforts to be successful, teachers, parents, community and business partners, administrators, and students must share leadership functions. Likewise, the principal's role must change from that of a top-down supervisor to a facilitator, architect, steward, instructional leader, coach, and strategic teacher (Senge, 1990).

Leading successful change and improvement involves developing and managing six critical components of schooling:

1 a clear, strong, and collectively held educational vision and institutional mission;
2 a strong, committed professional community within the school;
3 learning environments that promote high standards for student achievement;
4 sustained professional development to improve learning;
5 successful partnerships with parents, health and human service agencies, businesses, universities, and other community organizations; and
6 a systematic planning and implementation process for instituting needed changes.

Louis and Miles (1990), drawing on several case studies of urban high schools, emphasize the importance of planning: "Substantial change programs do not run themselves. They need active orchestration and coordination." (Peterson)

We can also obtain some insight from Paul Preuss, who says,

I have been misdirected enough times by so called instructional technology experts over the 36 years of my educational experience to become extremely wary of such "expert" input. I have found that getting information from a great variety of sources, and from all segments of the organization, and learning from others outside of the

I&T Team Snapshot from Timber Drive

"We've worked our way on this path every day for the past five years, and we will never stop. Once you get over the illusion that you may someday *arrive* at technology integration, and realize that improvement is forever, it becomes quite exciting. We all say *this is a work in progress* and I hope we never stop saying it."

— Mrs. Sue King - Pilot (Principal)

organization, are all necessary for reaching a sound decision. Although I do not consider myself a technologist - I do think that I have been successful in many instances of technological implementation in the places I have served. Most recently, for example, I was responsible for the development of a LAN which ultimately contained over 150 instructional and administrative work stations. Obviously - I had a lot of help - but the development of the LAN required much more human interaction and development than it did technical. (Preuss, "Caution")

3.3.1 Technology Standards for School Administrators

The vision of the TSSA Collaborative is that the Technology Standards for School Administrators identify knowledge and skills that constitute the "core" - what every P-12 administrator needs regardless of specific job role - and, then extends the core to include the specific tasks of administrators in each of three job roles: (1) superintendent and executive cabinet, (2) district-level leaders for content-specific or other district programs, and (3) campus-level leaders, including principals and assistant principals.

According to Don Knezek, Director of the TSSA Standards Project, "Integrating technology throughout a school system is, in itself, significant systemic reform. We have a wealth of evidence attesting to the importance of leadership in implementing and sustaining systemic reform in schools. It is critical, therefore, that we attend seriously to leadership for technology in schools." (TSSA)

3.3.2 TSSA: One Principal's View by Marguerite Baca, Principal, E.J. Martinez Elementary School

First of all, I believe in standards. I am a pretty new administrator, having completed my first year as principal of an elementary school in Santa Fe, New Mexico. We use our district and state standards, and, last summer, I was involved in writing the technology standards for our district. I was the only administrator working with five teachers integrating technology in their classrooms. I learned a great deal from them. I hadn't integrated technology in a lesson since I was a teacher, 4 years previously!

I believe that we all need standards. The Technology Standards for School Administrators Project has many powerful ideals. Of course I wish I were Wonder Woman, but no principal can do all this herself.

As far as the first requirements for technology to benefit our schools are concerned, hardware is not useful in itself. We have seen this in the past decade again and again. The applications and wiring added to the hardware make them useful to some-but only some. Too many unused computers have become thousand-dollar paperweights.

Equity is the biggest issue here. The "haves" and the "have-not's" in this instance are the teachers who *have* had training and those who *have not*, the teachers who *can* apply the training and those who *cannot*, and those who *have* time to "mouse around" versus those who *do not* or *will not*. Many if not all of the teachers who are computer savvy have become so on their own time. Evenings, summers, and other non-contract time is the only time available for teachers to learn what is essentially another language.

The capability of the administrator in effective integration of technology is critical. Inspiring leadership can't happen in a vacuum. The effective principal must trust and rely on the children, staff, and parents to build the vision together. All types of technology must be used to communicate this vision widely. The principal needs help in modeling innovative uses, working with teachers and students on projects showing one's own learning and creative potential. I believe this is where TSSA will play a vital role.

3.4 Wearing the Scholar's Hat:
Managing Knowledge (Library Media Specialist)

Everything I know about information literacy, and the power of teachers collaborating with library media specialists, I learned from Janet Murray. When we first organized the Online Internet Institute in 1995, I already looked to Janet as a leader. We'd worked together on the CoSN/FARnet project, the first meeting of educational networking pioneers to provide input to the National Science Foundation as they strove to expand Internet access to the K-12 community. In her article, Janet describes the evolving role of the library media specialist and the media center as the information hub of the school. Her ideas are powerful and timeless.

3.4.1 Excerpts from "Librarians Evolving into Cybrarians"

Many teachers and administrators do not yet realize that librarians [library media specialists] have precisely the training and skills needed to implement information literacy skills in the curriculum. The traditional library school provided instruction in organizing information (cataloging), evaluating materials (selection), and formulating research questions (conducting reference interviews).

School library media specialists have a unique opportunity to adapt their professional skills to meet the challenges of the Information Age. As electronic access to information proliferates in schools, library media specialists can model the adventure of lifelong learning by teaching faculty and students how to search the Internet for pertinent information, evaluate the reliability of information retrieved, analyze and synthesize the information to construct personal meaning, and apply it to informed decision making. Library media centers can be transformed from static repositories of print and audiovisual materials into dynamic and evolving information technology centers.

3.4.1.1 New Roles for School Librarians

Meeting this challenge demands an understanding of the expanded role of the library media specialist in schools. *Information Power* (ALA) defines four roles for the effective library media specialist. That the library media specialist is a *teacher* is well understood by those who have met their states' certification requirements, but not as well understood by other teachers and administrators. Although they do not preside over a self-contained classroom, library media specialists are an integral part of the students' learning experience. They help students and teachers define their information needs, locate information in a variety of formats, analyze and evaluate the information, and apply it to construct personal meaning.

Effective library media specialists are *instructional partners* with the teachers in their school. They collaborate with teachers to refine information-seeking assignments, encouraging the development of those that foster critical thinking. They identify the cross-curricular connections that are essential to interdisciplinary learning. They share their awareness of information, communication, and technology components of state and national standards to help teachers integrate them into their curriculum.

Librarians are *information specialists* and information generalists. They may not know the answer to a specific question, but they know where and how to find it. They select materials and electronic resources to support the curriculum and enrich the information environment of the school. They provide leadership in the adoption and use of information technologies.

Finally, library media specialists are *program administrators* who establish policies and procedures in their media or information technology centers, introduce new technologies to access information, balance their expenditures between print and other resources, and manage the use of facilities and equipment.

The Department of Defense Dependent Schools renamed their library media specialists "information specialists" and incorporated the other three roles described in *Information Power* into the major duties of their new position description:

As *teacher*, in collaboration with other educators, the information specialist assists members of the learning community with the integration of information literacy and information technology skills across the curriculum.

As *instructional partner*, the information specialist provides instructional leadership for educators and parents to integrate information literacy and technology experiences across the curriculum.

As *program administrator*, the information specialist develops, administers, assesses, and manages programs and facilities for the use of information resources and technologies.

3.4.1.2 Roles Related to Internet Use

The American Association of School Librarians (AASL) amplifies and clarifies these roles, particularly as they apply to Internet use, in its online resource, ICONnect.

- *Navigator*: Learn to navigate and effectively search the Internet.
- *Teacher and Collaborator*: Collaborate with teachers to design and implement authentic learning activities that utilize Internet resources.
- *Evaluator*: Develop evaluation tools and actively integrate evaluation into the curriculum.
- *Publisher*: Create resource guides that assist students, teachers, administrators, and parents to find quality Internet sites that are relevant to the curriculum.
- *Program Administrator*: Work collaboratively with members of the learning community to develop program policies related to Internet use.
- *Staff Developer*: Take a lead role in teaching faculty and administration to use the Internet effectively and to integrate Internet use into the curriculum.
- *Family Resource*: Promote positive and creative uses of the Internet to families.

ICONnect also provides electronic "tours" to help librarians become skillful in these roles.

Both *Information Power* and the DoDDS' job description emphasize the importance of technology in the librarian's evolving role. As information access becomes increasingly computerized, the school library media specialist will be responsible for introducing new technologies to her teaching colleagues and students, enabling and empowering them to adopt information literacy strategies to become independent lifelong learners.

3.5 Wearing the Guide's Hat: Managing Learners (Teacher Leader)

The teacher leader is like the tip of the proverbial iceberg. As remarkable as the appearance of a mountain of ice floating in the sea may be, it is the implication of the other nine-tenths, submerged, out of view, that is most awe-inspiring. It is also this unseen part that will sink reform efforts quicker than you can say "Titanic." In other words, for every pioneering educator you see using technology in innovative ways in your school, in magazines, and on the web, there are nine others who are in varying stages of reluctance and/or resistance. This is not news, but the characteristics shared by different kinds of teachers can provide us with information to develop strategies to reach every teacher, thereby reaching every child.

Although there was no name for it at the time, I've recently realized that I spent most of my career in education as a teacher leader. I didn't do things the same way as my peers, not from my first day as a music teacher to the last as a computer teacher. Rather than be guided by conformity, I pursued whatever worked best for my students. Sometimes this brought me into conflict with policies, practices and attitudes that could best be summed up as "that's the way we do things around here" with the unstated admonition "so don't rock the boat."

This didn't stop me from wanting to share the joy of

> **Carnegie Challenge 2002: Teaching as a Clinical Profession: A New Challenge for Education**
>
> Assess, diagnose, prescribe and adjust practice to reflect new research, training and experience - that 's what a modern clinical professional does. The job description not only fits physicians who see patients in clinics, it precisely defines the work of teachers who see students in classrooms. To many Americans, the analogy may smack of *Ripley's Believe It or Not*, for the shocking truth is that teachers need to know and be able to do far more than the nation understands or appreciates. (Hinds)

learning every day, right along with my kids, regardless of their age or mine. I'd try to engage my colleagues in team projects, or introduce them to resources, and found that some were willing to accept these invitations, while others were relentless in their desire to go it alone. I'm willing to wager that most of the readers of this book can resonate with this experience ... certainly most of the contributors do!

The benefits of educational technology do not occur in a vacuum; instead they flourish in an environment that reinforces research-based recommendations for improving education as a whole. While these recommendations may be controversial in some settings, both technology friends and foes agree that the most important person in education is the teacher. Therefore, isn't the most critical goal to provide the most effective, best-prepared teachers possible?

Data from the 1998 Teaching, Learning and Computing Survey (TLC) provides substantive insights about what is required to do so. In *The Beliefs, Practices, and Computer Use of Teacher Leaders*, Margaret Riel and Hank Becker describe a spectrum of classroom practice. This research analyzes the responses of 4,000 U. S. teachers concerning their educational background, teaching philosophy and instructional practices both with and without computers.

> At the high end of the continuum of levels of Professional Engagement are Teacher Leaders - teachers who place a high value on sharing their knowledge with their teaching colleagues. At the opposite end of the continuum are Private Practice Teachers who report little or no engagement in professional dialog or activities beyond those mandated. Teacher Professionals, similar to Teacher Leaders, were engaged beyond the classroom but reported less leadership activities. Interactive Teachers were not quite as disengaged as Private Practice Teachers. (Riel)

One of their dramatic findings was that teachers who have been identified as teacher leaders in their schools, in their districts and in their fields, were ten times more likely to be teachers who used computers themselves and have integrated the use of computers with their classroom instruction. These *teacher leaders*, teachers with a high degree of professional engagement and respect, contrasted with a group of teachers that Riel and Becker refer to as *private practice teachers*. This group of teachers had much lower investment in their own learning in pre-service education and in later years. When the private practice teachers did use computers, they did so in ways that supported drill and practice games. The evidence shows that teachers who invest heavily in their own learning are discovering how to teach effectively with computers, using them for problem solving, analysis and presentation. Riel and Becker continue,

> The findings are consistent and strong - Teacher Leaders are better educated teachers, continuous learners, computer users, and promote constructive problem-based learning over direct instruction. Their position in the educational community mirrors students' positions in their classrooms. They use computers to help their students achieve the same level of respect and voice that these teachers have achieved within their professional educational community.

My review of the TLC study and related research helped me understand the issues as follows: the knowledge transmission view of learning emphasizes teacher-centered whole-class explanation and closely scripted student seatwork. Classroom teachers who define instruction as the transmission of knowledge have students learn concepts and skills through listening, copying text, and practicing sets of similar problems. Classroom teachers who define instruction as the co-construction of knowledge focus on project activities that expect students to display understanding, interpretation, and original thought.

Models of school reform, professional development programs, state and federal policies increasingly support teachers in expanded roles, including as Teacher Leaders. Teacher Leaders and Teacher Professionals share constructivist philosophy and practice. They view teaching and learning as a co-constructive process in which students are asked to think deeply about issues, generate their own ideas, work collaboratively in projects, and share and evaluate their work within a public classroom forum. (Riel)

What is evident from comparing the educational background of professionally engaged and disengaged teachers is that teacher leaders have made and are continuing to make a substantial investment in their own education. These teacher characteristics - their education, ability, and experience - have been strongly associated with significant increases in student achievement.

The second finding is one that we want to underscore. Even when teachers shared similar beliefs concerning an active student role in constructing deep knowledge through collaborative project-based work, Teacher Leaders and Teacher Professionals were more effective than Private Practice or Interactive Teachers in translating these beliefs into practice. Teacher Leaders were 10 times more likely to be highly active computer users when compared to Private Practice teachers. They view computers as tools to help students to research, understand, and explain their ideas through text and graphics. (Riel)

3.5.1 Technology Standards for Teachers

The third edition of the *National Educational Technology Standards for Teachers (NETS-T)* reflects a comprehensive restructuring of the earlier versions, organizing 23 indicators into six categories aligned with the standards for students (NETS-S). The document's authors assert that

Traditional educational practices no longer provide prospective teachers with all the necessary skills for teaching students, who must be able to survive economically in today's workplace. Teachers must teach students to apply strategies for solving problems and to use appropriate tools for learning, collaborating, and communicating. (NETS-T)

The "primary goal" of the NETS project initiated by the International Society for Technology in Education (ISTE) was "to develop national standards for the educational uses of technology that facilitate school improvement in the United States." The authors conclude, "Today's classroom teachers must be prepared to provide technology-supported learning opportunities for their students."

3.6 Wearing the Hard Hat: Managing Resources (Technical Specialist)

In his article, Rob Reilly describes his role as the technology coordinator in a small district, but his observations are equally valid for the individual school's technical specialist. Reilly reports that he was "faced with the option of continuing as the school district's technology coordinator or returning to the classroom. After 2 years as the school district's Technology Coordinator, I had come to realize that my expectations of the position and the reality of what needs to be done were at odds. I expected to be the curriculum leader, but became the electronic janitor." (39)

3.6.1 Excerpts from "The Technology Coordinator: Curriculum Leader or Electronic Janitor?"

My expectations of the position and what the position really needed seemed not to be a unique experience. As Dr. Shiela Kieran-Greenbush from Teacher's College at Columbia University in New York City puts it, as Technology Coordinator, one person is being asked to "teach, design courses, keep up with technology, fix microcomputers, fix LAN networks, monitor and fix WANs, be a network administrator, be a WWW administrator, be an Internet guru, be a help desk, evaluate software and hardware, find and get grants, and generally do what an academic computing department in a small college would do."

Based upon my experiences and conversations with my colleagues, it is evident that any hope a newly hired Technology Coordinator has of becoming the technology leader-the technology curriculum guru-vanishes in the first few months of their tenure and tends to never return.

If a Technology Coordinator is to have any hope of successfully facilitating curriculum integration and technology literacy for the staff and students and providing for effective tactical and strategic planning, this person must have a firm plan in-hand and be certain that the expectations of the school system match. To avoid many of the pitfalls, I suggest that the Technology Coordinator must first and foremost be prepared in the following ways:

- Have a goal that is similar to the school system's technology goal (or convince them to "buy into" your goal). I'd suggest that a Technology Coordinator's goal might be to fully integrate technology into a school system that has the resources and desire to move forward toward the technological demands of the 21st century school system.
- Have a personal perspective in regard to technology that provides a vision and reflects a leadership persona. A good perspective is that many schools today have (or should be deploying) computer labs, computers in classrooms, a LAN, the Internet, and facilitating teachers into becoming ready and willing to embrace technology.
- Be able to answer the question, "How many people do we need if one is NOT enough?" As Educational Technology Planner at the Board of Cooperative Education (BOCES) for western New York, Margaret Dyte-Graczyk says that...when her department is called in to help a district plan for technology, "We recommend hiring a team of three, minimum: a tech coordinator to run the whole department and oversee the budget, researching and keeping up with the changes in technology, ordering of equipment, etc.; a technical person to install it all, troubleshoot, and keep

it running; and a technology integrator to help with the training and, more importantly, implementing the integration of technology into the curriculum with an emphasis on standards, etc."
• Do NOT become the break-fix person-the Electronic Janitor.

The Technology Coordinator's Plan of Action must also include these points in order to preclude becoming the dreaded Electronic Janitor:

• Develop and conduct technology professional development;
• Develop, supervise, and facilitate technology integration into the curriculum;
• Develop a district-wide continuity plan for technology (administration, business, and classroom);
• Have a firm understanding of the salary and benefits package and of the nature of the position-e.g., administrative position, faculty position.

In closing, allow me to suggest that a school system must decide what the nature of the position is going to be, as Dr. Kieran-Greenbush well states: "K-12 has to understand that one or two people cannot do everything. You have to decide what is important and have them do only that." If a Technology Coordinator does not meticulously define their position, that person may as well hang a "Cinderella" sign on their office door.

Dr. G. Ernest Anderson of the University of Massachusetts wonders aloud if his efforts in "trying to prepare people for positions that should be there but which have not developed yet was simply a decade too early." Anderson, who was a Western Union telegraph operator in the '40s, muses, "Perhaps technology is correctly viewed as an add-on skill for educators who are doing other things rather than a worthwhile specialty in itself." Anderson does see the situation changing but wonders, "Who will provide leadership, and where will these people be located in the education hierarchy?" He believes that "time will tell."

3.7 Conclusion: Winning Teams Know Their Roles

Is our teaching effective? Who's being left behind? Which skills must our teachers master next, in order to help students move ahead? How can we prepare students for mandated assessments without tunnel-vision teaching-to-the-test? How can we begin to collect benefit from the dollars we've invested in education technology? How are we going to get the money, the time, and the talented people we need to sustain improvement?

Questions like these are the fuel that propels I&T Teams at schools where information technology works in service of learning. Meeting the challenges of *No Child Left Behind* is fundamentally an information-based problem. The people with the expertise to address this problem are already at your school: the principal, library media specialist, teacher leaders and technical specialists. As in sports, each position has a specific assignment, but no matter how skilled the individuals, they will never combine to form a championship team unless every player understands the roles of the other players and how they relate to each other. Now that we've studied each other's roles, Chapter Four will guide you to building the relationships and expertise required to thrive in 21st Century learning environments.

Key Conversations:

**How I&T Teams
Manage Change**

4.1 Overview

The power of I&T Teams comes from the potential to focus FITness (contemporary skills, foundational concepts and intellectual capabilities) upon a common vision, to address building level challenges. In order for the I&T Team to manage change, they must initiate and support ongoing key conversations, focused around four purposes: **Accountability, Learning, Leadership** and **Technical**.

The team members must arrive at a shared understanding about the first three (accountability, learning and leadership), before any consideration of technical issues can be useful. Collectively, members of the I&T Team touch every facet of school activity at the building level. Therefore, it is important to organize these conversations so that the team members' efforts align to support the distinct, yet interrelated objectives of each of them. Because the decision making related to each of these purposes involves different aspects of school operations, we've assembled the groups differently for each conversation.

When we are trying to satisfy state and federal requirements (**Accountability**), we're thinking about compliance. When we are considering how best to prepare students for the 21st century (**Learning**), we're focusing on instructional strategies that help them acquire contemporary literacy skills for lifelong learning. When we are planning to move the entire staff toward contemporary literacy (**Leadership**), we must consider professional development as well as teach by example. Finally, when we are deciding how to implement an infrastructure capable of supporting everyone in the learning community (**Technical**), money and staffing come into the picture.

> ## I&T Team Snapshot from Timber Drive
>
> "It is crucial that an appropriate culture be in place. The culture must support professionalism enough to set a standard for being innovative and willing to change methods in order to improve."
> Frank Creech - CoPilot (Assistant Principal)

In each of the following sections, we offer suggestions about what each member of the I&T Team brings (or needs to bring) to the table. Then the questions listed under conversations help bring issues into focus.

4.2 Accountability: Making IT Work for Assessment and Growth

Regardless of how we may feel about mandated, annual high-stakes testing, the accountability provisions of *No Child Left Behind* will be part of our reality for the foreseeable future. Compliance with these accountability requirements presents a complex challenge. Although the focus is on the individual child (particularly those children who fall into a series of subgroups whose lack of success have historically been masked by the "average" performance of students as a whole), the unit of measure and target of consequences is the school itself. In far too many schools, the threat of consequences imposed because of low scores on mandated statewide high-stakes tests has resulted in "teaching to the test," thereby narrowing the curricular focus.

Meeting these challenges is fundamentally a knowledge management problem: information concerning the progress of subgroups specified in the legislation exists at your school, but it is typically fragmented and difficult to synthesize into meaningful trends. For example, data must be disaggregated into the following subgroups:

- Gender,
- Each major racial and ethnic group,
- English proficiency status,
- Migrant status,
- Students with disabilities compared to all other students,
- Economically disadvantaged students compared to students who are not economically disadvantaged. (Clements)

It is one thing to know how many students you have in each of these groups. It is quite another to know who they are, and what their teachers are doing to prepare them to succeed on the tests. Since the unit of measure for accountability is the school, the principal, as **pilot**, owns responsibility for these actions. The I&T Team members who can help the most in applying the power of technology to this knowledge management problem are the **scholar** (library media specialist) and the **guide** (teacher leader). These are the roles and responsibilities each member of the accountability conversation can contribute.

I&T Team Snapshot from Timber Drive

"Each year, when the state testing data arrives, we hire subs and spend time with teachers, looking at the data, child by child. A team comprised of every professional who works with any child who's having difficulty confers about patterns we see in the data. We do not focus on remediation; we believe that an invigorating experience of learning is good for every child. There are multiple opportunities for each child to learn a concept; they may learn it with Steve in the lab, with Nancy in the media center, in class. We have such abilities to differentiate instruction, to use different media and modalities to get the concepts across (through the Big6 and WebQuests) that we provide opportunities for all to grow."

"An example is our Write Point project. When this school opened, we drew from 13 sending schools. That first year our scores on the 4th Grade NC writing assessment left us no doubt we had a problem! Children came to us with 13 different levels of preparation. We experimented with a program of concentrated writing instruction. We brought in all the specialists (media, technology, administrators, special ed) and created a cadre of writing coaches. We took the entire fourth grade population and divided them, by ability, among the staff, which resulted in groups of about eight students per staff. We zeroed in on the needs for each specific group, using this approach: what is our problem, what do we want to happen, what can we do to get there? The results were incredible, and set us on our path for continuous growth."

Mrs. Sue King - Pilot (Principal)

4.2.1 Pilot Contributions

As instructional leader of the school, the principal will have the most direct access to testing data provided by the district. Examining performance trends at the classroom and student level by analyzing multiple years of performance can highlight gaps that need to be addressed. However, this one-dimensional picture doesn't provide sufficient richness to guide improvement. Data from multiple measures comes from the other members of this conversation.

4.2.2 Scholar Contributions

The scholar (library media specialist) is trained as an information professional, and can organize both the search for resources, as well as the information that is retrieved. The library media specialist is also the only person on the staff who partners with every educator in the building, and therefore has the most comprehensive view of the curriculum as taught. The library media specialist can see what is being done for students in these subgroups as they flow through the instructional program at your school. Data about which resources are being used, how students are improving at skills of comprehension and synthesis (two key factors in performing on any assessment instrument), and the literacy levels of materials being used by students are all within the reach of the scholar. However, without the cooperation of the principal in terms of scheduling (supporting the desire for active involvement with the entire staff) and designing appropriate staff development activities, the library media specialist's talents often go unrealized.

4.2.3 Guide Contributions

The guide (teacher leader) has a complementary role. The state mandated tests may happen only once a year, but there are many more frequent opportunities to look at the results of instruction. The teacher leader and the library media specialist can design strategies for collecting and interpreting student performance data. As the instructional implementation leader, the guide is most conversant with strategies to reach diverse learners, and best able to coach other teachers in their classrooms. Suggestions for improvement that emerge from the accountability conversations can only be incorporated over time, in classrooms. Guided by teacher and student performance trends, informed by opportunities to collaborate with the library media specialist, the teacher leader can focus on specific interventions with other staff members. However, unless supported by scheduling and resource decisions made by the principal, school wide improvement efforts remain elusive.

I&T Team Snapshot from Timber Drive

"Too often when people focus on data and test scores, they lose sight of the primary resource for improving achievement: building relationships and community. Our administrators took a risk, in allowing us to devote extra resources to building our team. It is a risk that has paid off. Of the 78 elementary schools in our district, Timber Drive is one of eleven schools that has met both Expected and High Growth standards for five consecutive years. This didn't happen through remediation. It happened by strengthening learning for all students."

Steven Moore - Guide
(Teacher Leader, Instructional Technology Facilitator)

6• Getting Started: Assessment - What's Going On?

"Feedback is information about what happened, the result or effect of our actions. ... Guidance, on the other hand, gives future direction: what should I do, in light of what just happened? And evaluation, finally, judges my overall performance against a standard. Feedback tells me whether I am on course. Guidance tells me the most likely ways to achieve my goal. Evaluation tells me whether I am or have been sufficiently on course to be deemed competent or successful." (Wiggins)

Read Grant Wiggins' essay "Feedback: How Learning Occurs." <http://www.relearning.org/resources/PDF/feedback.pdf> As a team, discuss the following questions:

1 How does technology currently provide feedback that is useful to learners and teachers?

2 How might technology be used to provide additional feedback that is useful to learners and teachers?

Complete the matrix below to see where each I&T Team member can contribute to the strengthening of your assessment capabilities:

Task	Wizard	Pilot	Scholar	Guide	Hard Hat
What feedback do you receive?					
What feedback do you provide?					
What evidence of staff technology use do you observe?					
What evidence of student technology use do you observe?					
How can you communicate your findings and make sure the staff you work with understand them?					

4.2.4 Accountability Conversations

- Who are the students in each accountability subgroup (gender, major racial and ethnic groups, limited English proficiency, migrant, disabilities and economically disadvantaged)?
- What are the performance trends for these groups and individuals on the three most recent measures?
- Which teachers are having the most and least success with these groups?
- Which areas and topics are students having the most difficulty mastering?
- Which teachers are having the most and least success with these topics?
- What research exists to guide interventions on these topics?
- What resources do we have, or could we acquire, to support these efforts?
- How can the I&T team contribute to lessening the detrimental effects and derive any possible benefits that can arise from demonstrating **adequate yearly progress** for our school?

4.2.5 Accountability Strategies: Making IT Work for Assessment and Growth

Tools such as *Data Connections: Using Assessments to Improve Teaching and Learning* represent a significant example of ways the I&T Team can foster accountability throughout the entire school. The I&T Team can help teachers analyze and interpret standardized test data, use data to plan for effective instruction, develop classroom assessments that align with standards, and prepare students to perform at their best on standardized tests.

I&T Team Snapshot from Timber Drive

Using data to guide instruction is nothing new to us in North Carolina. We've been doing this for the last five or six years with data from the North Carolina ABC's of Public Education (our State-wide standardized testing). Looking at data and changing what we're doing on the basis of needs the children are showing only makes sense. The NCDPI and our district research department provide us with disaggregated test data. We work with teachers to analyze this data. The flexibility of our team approach enables us to break large classes down into smaller groups, targeting skills and individual student needs.

Frank Creech, Susan Boyer
CoPilots (Assistant Principals)

7• Getting Started:
Accountability - Meeting Targeted Goals

"Assessment should be used for three distinct purposes: 1) as a basis for making modifications while the course is in progress (formative evaluation); 2) as verification that individual students have gained knowledge or skills (certification); and 3) as an indicator of the extent to which the course has effectively met its goals (summative evaluation)." (Ragan)

In order to understand the needs of children targeted by the accountability provisions of NCLB, and how their use of technology strengthens their academic performance, your team will need to develop answers to the following questions:

1 Who are the students in each accountability subgroup (gender, major racial and ethnic groups, limited English proficiency, migrant, disabilities and economically disadvantaged)?

2 Which teachers do they work with?

3 How is your school using the data from state mandated and school/district initiated periodic assessments to identify the academic needs of students in each subgroup?

4 How well does your choice of standardized test provide the kind of data that will help improve learning in your district?

Score your standardized test on these seven criteria to determine its ability to provide the kind of data that will help improve learning in your district. For each item, score one through five, according to the scale for each. When you have finished, compare your total to the chart to see how your test rates.

1 The test is accurate for *every* student.

    1 Not accurate for any
    2
    3 Accurate for average students
    4
    5 Accurate for 95% to 100% of students

2 The test results provide instructionally useful information.

    1 Not useful
    2
    3 Somewhat useful
    4
    5 Extremely useful

3 The test measures growth over time. It tracks student learning or progress across grades.

    1 Does not measure growth
    2
    3 Measures growth only within grades
    4
    5 Measures growth across grades

4 Test results are available within five days of testing.

    1 Results never arrive
    2
    3 Results arrive within 3 months
    4
    5 Results available in 5 days or fewer

5 The test is aligned with state content and/or goal standards.

    1 Not aligned
    2
    3 Somewhat aligned
    4
    5 Aligned

6 The test data are useful for a variety of audiences (teachers, parents, administrators, and school board members).

    1 Not useful
    2
    3 Useful for district personnel only
    4
    5 Useful for all

7 The test provides external accountability (e.g., it is norm referenced).

    1 No accountability
    2
    3 Some accountability
    4
    5 Fully accountable

Scoring

5-14 Your district's testing program may not be telling you what you need to know about learning in your student population. You may also be at risk for meeting the requirements of the *No Child Left Behind* legislation. You would benefit from talking to an assessment organization that can help you meet your data goals.

15-27 You are seeing some value from your testing program but you could do better. You would benefit from talking to an assessment organization to learn how you can maximize the tests you have and to learn about new testing options that would help your district meet its achievement goals.

28-35 Your district's testing program is in good shape as long as you're testing what you want to know. You would benefit from talking to an assessment organization to maximize the tests you are currently using and to conduct an annual evaluation of your program.

Score analysis provided courtesy of the Northwest Evaluation Association.

4.3 Learning: Harnessing the Power of IT

It is important not to confuse accountability with learning. Learning in the 21st century goes far beyond the "cutoff score" design of accountability measures, as well as the capabilities of existing measurement tools. We must design for this higher standard, to properly serve every child and strengthen every school. Curriculum mapping is an important activity to align the efforts of every teacher in every classroom in the school.

8• Getting Started:
Curriculum Mapping - Charting Your Way to Success

Curriculum Mapping is a process that educators use to develop a calendar that shows the content, skills, and assessments that students experience at each grade level in a school. This calendar is particularly useful for making visible the missing pieces and the duplications as a student goes from grade to grade. A systematic examination of the curriculum and upcoming assessments allows us to allocate time on the calendar to make sure that our students have the experiences required to learn the content and master the skills for which they will be held accountable.

Now it's time to understand what is (and is not) actually happening at your school. As a team, create a curriculum map:

1 What is being taught in each classroom, by semester, month and week?

2 What classroom assessments are correlated with the content to measure student mastery of standards?

3 What experiences do students have with technology to support this learning, by semester, month and week?

From *Constructivist-Compatible Beliefs and Practices among U.S. Teachers*

Our data suggests that academic subject-matter teachers who use computers most productively in grades 4-12 are not very comfortable with a transmission-oriented pedagogy, even though that is the approach which may satisfy policy-makers and large portions of the public through realizing higher standardized test scores. These teachers, instead, implicitly if not explicitly, endorse an alternative philosophy of teaching, which might be explained as including two pedagogical emphases:

- attending to the "meaningfulness" of instructional content for each student - for example by developing examples connected to students' own personal experience or by providing opportunities for students to present detailed explanations of their reasoning
- developing students' capacities to understand a subject deeply enough, and see the interrelationships of different ideas and issues, so they are able to know how and when to apply their knowledge to particular contexts and communicate their understandings to others.

Constructivist theory claims that understanding comes from a person's taking the effort to integrate newly communicated claims and ideas with his own prior beliefs and understandings. In that view, understanding cannot be transmitted, nor does skills-practice result in understanding which can be automatically applied as needed. Instead, good teaching involves creating environments in which students take mindful effort towards developing their understanding, and have opportunities to learn how to apply their knowledge and when to do so. (Ravitz)

At the building level, the I&T team members who can most directly shape technology's contributions to learning are the **scholar** (library media specialist), the **guide** (teacher leader) and the **hard hat** (technical specialist). They can make sure that the technology works to support 21st century learning, by incorporating the findings of the *Teaching, Learning and Computing* study.

4.3.1 Scholar Contributions

The school library media specialist has had the benefit of extensive training that other educators have not. The skills acquired in library school (finding, organizing, evaluating, and managing information) are precisely those that are needed when educators turn to the Internet seeking materials from which they can craft effective learning experiences. It is often said, "if the World Wide Web had been invented by librarians instead of physicists, we'd not have most of the problems we're faced with today" in terms of infoglut and

> ## I&T Team Snapshot from Timber Drive
>
> "Trust is crucial. The trust level must be deep enough that we can focus on teaching how to learn, not what to learn. Collaboration at this level is not tied into planning periods, where kids come to the lab or media center to provide teachers with a break. We're in there together, working together for the benefit of the kids.
>
> Teachers come to us, suggesting topics, and we help them to design lessons, many times teaching the lessons with them. Word soon gets around, and other teachers want to know if we can teach those lessons with their classes. Soon, these good practices spread throughout the school."
>
> Nancy Finger, Sue Ellen Ott - Scholars
> (Library Media Specialists)

infotrash. (See Jamie McKenzie's *From Now On* website for a series of provocative and insightful essays on this and related topics.)

4.3.2 Guide Contributions

The teacher leader, often working alone, invests significant time in developing activities tailored to the needs of his class, balancing the scope and sequence with opportunities to build knowledge, to deepen his students' learning. However, nowhere in his professional training, has he been exposed

---

I&T Team Snapshot from Timber Drive

"Our staff development happens before school. In my position as network administrator, I am able to offer staff development during the teacher's planning time as well - one on one or small group instruction. Although Steven has a schedule, and can't be as flexible as I can in working directly with teachers and students, we do find ways to work with them, in the lab, in the media center, in classrooms, in the TV studio. With the recent addition of LCD projectors for each grade level we are able to support teachers as they integrate technology into their classrooms and their lessons in ways they couldn't do before. It takes lots of the pressure and fear off of them when we're able to be there, alongside teachers in preparation for their lessons."

Ted Fillhart - Guide, Hard Hat (Teacher Leader, Network Administrator)

---

to the concepts of information literacy, nor guided on how to gain the most from the assistance that the library media specialist is ready and willing to provide.

4.3.3 Hard Hat Contributions

The I&T team engages in conversations that can be facilitated by the network, if the technical specialist makes it possible. For example, curriculum maps can become living documents, available to all, and updated by each participant, to form the focal point for powerful conversations. Learning conversations establish the technical specialist's priorities to support these collaborative uses of network resources.

I&T Team Snapshot from Timber Drive

"It's no secret that I have a unique position as a network administrator (system operator) at an elementary school. It is so important for someone who's hired for a position like mine to be a certified teacher. I was a classroom teacher for 14 years before taking on this position 3.5 years ago. Why is being teacher in my position so crucial? I am able to relate to teachers and understand what their needs are. Those needs range from what needs to be fixed, who needs to be trained, what application would work best, and so on. Not only do I work with the network, but as a certified teacher I can actually teach a 5th grade language arts class, or lead a 4th grade small group in microscopic organisms or share a book talk with kindergartners."

Ted Fillhart - Hard Hat, Guide (Network Administrator, Teacher Leader)

4.3.4 Learning Conversations

- How can we make it possible for every student and every teacher to access their work from anywhere?
- How many people can use the network at one time?
- What information do we need to set up collaborative areas or projects?
- How much lead time do we need to set up such collaborative areas/projects?
- How can we make sure students and teachers have access to sites that may be incorrectly blocked by our filtering system?
- What will be our procedure for publishing student and teacher projects on the web?
- What upcoming topics and activities are teachers planning?
- How will we locate, use and evaluate information to support these activities?
- What can we do to make sure the students know how to find and select appropriate resources?
- How can we incorporate information literacy standards into these activities?
- How can we improve our research assignments to incorporate critical thinking skills?

I&T Team Snapshot from Timber Drive

"The kids who come to us at or below grade level grow the fastest. Students near the top require support in problem solving, to build higher order thinking skills. That's where the Big6 has been so helpful. A tremendous number of curriculum goals can be addressed in a single project when we can differentiate instruction in such ways."

Frank Creech, Susan Boyer - CoPilots
(Assistant Principals)

- How can we collaborate to plan effective learning experiences?
- How can we use the available data to improve student achievement?

4.3.5 Learning Strategies: Harnessing the Power of IT

The Big6™ Skills process provides a useful framework for these conversations because it can be applied to any task or problem whose solution requires information. Conversations between the library media specialist and the teacher leader that use the Big6 as a common language will inform the curriculum development process as well as identify topics for ongoing staff development. The first section also describes how students can approach "Fluency with Information Technology" by placing these skills within the Big6 context.

Carmean and Haefner describe the research basis for "deeper learning principles." Evidence from the Plano (TX) Independent School District demonstrates how data can be gathered, interpreted and applied to improve student achievement.

4.3.6 Excerpts from "Beyond the Bells and Whistles: Technology Skills for a Purpose"

The Big6 provides the framework for learning and applying technology. Individual information and technology skills take on new meaning when they are integrated within the Big6, and students develop true "computer literacy" because they have genuinely applied various computer and technology skills as part of the learning process.

Moving from teaching isolated computer skills to helping students learn integrated information and technology skills is not just a good idea. It's essential if we are to put students in a position to succeed in an increasingly complex and changing world. (46)

When you reflect on integrating technology skills into teaching and learning, you realize that it is not necessary to change the fundamentals of quality instruction or the information problem-solving perspective that is at the heart of this approach. The implementation of technology through the Big6 works in the following ways:

- It develops students' problem-solving, complex thinking, and information management abilities.
- It enables students to become comfortable with technology and understand that the technologies are valuable tools to help them perform their work.
- It focuses students' attention on using technologies as tools to extend knowledge and to individualize learning.

- It develops an active participatory learning process in which students become self-directed learners.
- It facilitates integrating technology across all grades and into all disciplines.
- It assists teachers to change their roles from presenters of information to "learning coaches" who offer tools and advice.
- It helps teachers introduce technology and have students use technologies even if the teachers aren't experts themselves. (50)

4.3.7 Excerpts from "Mind over Matter: Transforming Course Management Systems into Effective Learning Environments"

Can the tools themselves facilitate deeper learning? As increasing numbers of higher education and K-12 schools turn to online learning environments, Learning Management Systems (LMS) and Course Management Systems (CMS), we are well advised to turn to research rather than folk wisdom. In "Mind over Matter: Transforming Course Management Systems into Effective Learning Environments," Colleen Carmean and Jeremy Haefner synthesize various research theories on learning into five core learning principles. - FS

Our principles are directed at what we call *deeper learning* - an engaged learning that results in a meaningful understanding of material and content. This deeper learning experience occurs when learning is

- *social,*
- *active,*
- *contextual,*
- *engaging, and*
- *student-owned.*

Although deeper learning occurs with these five principles, they need not be present either all the time or all at once.

4.3.7.1 What is the Research Basis for Deeper Learning Principles?

Advances in learning research have significantly enhanced the current understanding of learning. In our own effort to understand how today's CMS can be used to create rich learning environments, we focused on the following works: John D. Bransford, Ann L. Brown, and Rodney R. Cocking, eds., *How*

Table 1. Deeper Learning Principles		
Learning is ...	**When ...**	**Summarized from:**
Social	It involves cognitive apprenticeship. It promotes reciprocity and cooperation among students. It offers prompt feedback. It encourages contact between students and faculty. It emphasizes rich, timely feedback.	Brown Chickering and Ehrmann Chickering and Ehrmann Chickering and Ehrmann Marchese
Active	It is engaged in solving real-world problems. It is intertwined in judgment and exploration. It is situated in action. It uses active learning techniques. Practice and reinforcement are emphasized. Involvement in real-world tasks is emphasized.	Merrill Brown Brown Chickering and Ehrmann Marchese Marchese
Contextual	New knowledge builds on the learner's existing knowledge. New knowledge is integrated into the learner's world. Knowledge is applied by the learner. New knowledge is demonstrated to the learner. Students have a deep foundation of factual knowledge. There is awareness that students come to the classroom with preconceptions about how the world works. Students understand facts and ideas in the context of a conceptual framework. Learning is concrete rather than abstract.	Merrill Merrill Merrill Merrill Bransford, Brown, and Cocking Bransford, Brown, and Cocking Bransford, Brown, and Cocking Brown
Engaging	It respects diverse talents and ways of learning. It communicates high expectations. It is done in high-challenge, low-threat environments. It emphasizes intrinsic motivators and natural curiosities.	Chickering and Ehrmann Chickering and Ehrmann Marchese Marchese
Student-Owned	Students organize knowledge in ways that facilitate retrieval and application. Students take control of their own learning: noting failures, planning ahead, apportioning time and memory to tasks. It emphasizes time on task. It emphasizes learner independence and choice. It allows time for reflection. It emphasizes higher-order thinking (synthesis and reflection).	Bransford, Brown, and Cocking Bransford, Brown, and Cocking Chickering and Ehrmann Marchese Marchese Marchese

People Learn; John Seely Brown, "Growing Up Digital"; Arthur W. Chickering and Stephen C. Ehrmann, "Implementing the Seven Principles"; Theodore J. Marchese, "The New Conversations about Learning"; and W. David Merrill, "First Principles of Instruction." These authors present their own theories for effective learning, but they all touch on several overlapping and important concepts. Using these concepts as a basis, we have developed a core set of deeper learning principles, as presented in Table 1.

When well-constructed practices around these deeper learning principles are used within a CMS [course management system], incredibly robust and effective learning environments are created. For instance, the use of a discussion board in an asynchronous CMS is a combination of both the social and the engaging learning principles, and the result is a powerful opportunity not only to engage the student with the social nature of learning but also to encourage the student to take ownership in the learning process. Likewise, the use of multimedia-rich case studies not only is engaging and encourages ownership but also develops a contextual learning approach. These are only two examples of how a few well-crafted instructional activities can lead to a very rich, student-centered learning experience.(Carmean)

4.3.8 A Journey of Continuous Improvement

Moving from a basis of "that's the way we've always done it" to a process of continuous improvement informed by real data from real students may seem simple, until you try it. In June 2002, I attended a presentation describing the Plano (TX) Independent School District's incredible improvements in performance achieved by making such a journey. Plano ISD, a highly respected school district located approximately 20 miles north of Dallas, is nationally known for its curriculum, instruction, student performance and the integration of technology into the support of instruction. Plano ISD is home to 49,000 students and 6,500 employees in 59 schools. In 2001, "Plano ISD boasted 37 'exemplary' schools and received an overall district 'recognized' rating for the second consecutive year" from the Texas Education Agency. (For more on Plano ISD achievements see http://www.pisd.edu/

AOS/General/bluerib.htm) Their story provides a detailed view of the tools and concepts required for success in the current environment of data-driven decision-making.

After investigating what it would take to effectively and efficiently provide their administrators, principals, teachers, and support staff with the data they needed to impact student learning, Plano installed their first instructional management system. ABACUS functions as a technology-based file cabinet and retrieval system that houses norm referenced and criterion referenced test data for tests such as SAT, ACT, ITBS, CogAT, MAP and TAAS. Diagnostic test, district exam and performance task data also reside in ABACUS, so the system enables district and campus staff to view individual and group performance by student, classroom, teacher, grade, campus, and demographic groups. Individual test items are linked to the curriculum and to specific instructional objectives. ABACUS generates reports including item analysis as well as mastery information on student performance by objective.

Recently, Plano has upgraded from ABACUS to a totally integrated, user friendly, web-based instructional management system. EdSoft will allow the district to use online and scanned assessment capabilities in conjunction with disaggregated data and high stakes reporting tools to measure student achievement in real time. It will easily turn the resulting data into readily accessible user-defined reports with the ultimate benefit of making well-informed data-driven decisions to guide the instructional process. "We have been searching for a web-based tool having both a simple end-user interface and a depth of data mining," said Dr. Priscilla Kimery, the Director of Research, Assessment and Evaluation. "We believe the EdSoft tools will greatly enhance our school and district improvement planning."

Additionally, the high stakes reporting capability will enable all Plano professionals to easily upload their testing results for a number of tests such as TAAS, SAT, and CogAT. Once in the EdSoft framework, Plano administrators and teachers will then be able to view a variety of reports and graphs, from longitudinal district summary information to individual student results across multiple assessments. This information, in addition to district-delivered assessments, will provide an easy to use comparison and analytical tool to address student mastery. Enhanced graphing capabilities in the reporting and analysis module will allow Plano educators to quickly toggle between tables and graphs. In addition, Plano professionals can build reports to their specifications utilizing filters for demographic information, assessment years, and student cohort information spanning multiple years.

4.3.8.1 Analyzing Results for Growth

The Northwest Evaluation Association's Measures of Academic Progress (MAP) test provides teachers with specific and immediate feedback on individual student achievement. Students take computer adapted reading, math, and language tests tailored to individual achievement levels. As each student finishes a test, the immediately generated scale score helps teachers plan instructional programs, place new students, and screen students for special programs. After teachers upload student test results over the Internet, NWEA provides more detailed individual student, class, school, and district reports within twenty-four hours of receiving the upload.

For Plano ISD, technology is the vehicle that consolidates, illustrates, and communicates data and information necessary for educators in partnership with parents to positively impact student learning and performance. Since it is the teacher who has the most profound influence on student learning, each teacher has access to every piece of information that could possibly contribute to helping students succeed. Every day Plano ISD students benefit from the massive amount of data each teacher can access at the click of a mouse. District and campus support staff work with teachers to help them understand and use the information available to them. Using all the tools at their disposal, everyone in the district collaborates as a team to:

- support continuous improvement;
- determine to what extent students are achieving the expectations for their learning;

- determine to what extent instructional practices support student achievement;
- determine to what extent the organizational conditions of the school support student learning;
- identify priorities for improvement and streamline curriculum;
- incorporate a balanced variety of measures to be used in decision making;
- provide data to aid in campus and district decision making;
- analyze to what extent research-based best practices are reflected in a campus' work;
- identify perceived strengths and limitations of instructional practices and organizational conditions of each campus and within program areas;
- identify action steps for achieving campus and district goals;
- determine allotment of resources and alignment of personnel.

4.4 Leadership: Making IT Work to Provide Sustained Support

Leadership's first priority is to decide how to achieve the closely related objectives of **accountability** and **learning** to make the school a place where learning demonstrably exceeds accountability performance goals. In order for no school to be left behind, individual schools need to assemble resources, support and civic participation to accomplish these goals. Their successes also need to be translated to the district level. Similarly, challenges faced at the building level can often be solved for all schools by district-wide implementations and purchases. (Access to online curriculum and reference materials is a prime example.)

No Child Left Behind requires that 25% of all funds spent on technology be directed toward staff development. How should those resources be spent? Conversations of this nature must involve the **wizard** (for district policy, budgeting and implementation), the **pilot** (for allocating building resources) and the **scholar** (for curriculum mapping, staff development and technology integration perspectives).

9• Getting Started:
Learning - Aligning Vision and Practice

Our vision of contemporary literacy cuts across all grade levels and curriculum areas. Therefore, it is important to review every opportunity to enhance traditional practice with these new capabilities. You've already developed curriculum maps to identify what's actually happening in every classroom. You've looked at the needs of students most at risk of being left behind, and anticipated interventions that will help improve their performance on mandated tests. Now it's time to shift gears to reach the highest levels of learning, and determine the concrete actions your team will take to get there.

1. Now that you've reviewed the curriculum maps for your school, where are the most promising points to introduce information literacy activities at each grade level?

2. Which of the NETS (for students, teachers and administrators) do these activities address?

3. How will the interactions between the I&T team and the staff contribute to their mastery of required skills?

4. How does your network support communication and collaboration among and beyond the I&T team to share the results of applied contemporary literacy?

Complete the matrix below to see where each I&T Team member can contribute to moving from vision to practice:

Task	Wizard	Pilot	Scholar	Guide	Hard Hat
Articulating your vision to staff and students.					
Assessing current skill levels of staff and students.					
Designing adequate capacity for full participation by staff and students.					

4.4.1 Wizard Contributions

Aligning the district technology plan with needs at the building level requires the technology coordinator's perspective, especially with the national shift away from site-based purchasing decisions. Designing the network to support accountability, assessment, instruction and staff development requires a coordinated approach. However, the wizard's dual role in supporting administrative as well as instructional uses of technology often results in greater familiarity with "mission critical" (payroll, personnel, transmission of state required data) rather than curricular implications. Similarly, a division at the district level too often isolates curricular decisions from the benefit of insight into how technology might assist in reaching learning objectives.

Knowing what is happening at the building level as a result of implementing district policy is a key benefit of the technology coordinator's participation in the leadership conversation. Knowing what support is available from the district as well as state and federal funding is a key benefit to the school.

4.4.2 Pilot Contributions

The principal is the manager for overall school operations. Setting the tone for the community of professionals who comprise the school, making decisions about communication, scheduling, budgeting and staffing, the principal determines what progress happens intentionally, and what happens in spite of an absence of leadership. On the basis of the leadership conversation, the principal secures the support and resources to extend the benefits of technology to all learners in the school community.

Attracting and retaining staff who fit the profile of teacher leaders is important, but it is even more vital to move the rest of our respective staffs ahead through the stages from *private practice* to *interactive teachers* to

---

I&T Team Snapshot from Timber Drive

"*No Child Left Behind* is certainly proving to be a wake up call for many districts. They are being challenged to *do something different*. My message to these districts is this: a school's media/technology staff helps ensure that no child will be left behind. Schools that have decreased or dropped their Media programs are depriving themselves of just the resources they need to succeed. Our Media/Technology team is composed of the leaders of our instructional program. We constantly speak of the Library/ Media Center as the hub of learning at our school, and for us, that is more than just words.

Nancy, our library/media specialist, really did educate me. I was a classroom teacher, but I hadn't experienced the technology or the media. I was open to finding new and better ways to help children learn, so this was great to discover. At our previous school, we'd developed a model of collaborative planning and teaching, so with this model in place, we set about building our new school. This model embraces the integration of technology as a key tool for learning, a tool with incredible resources embedded."

Mrs. Sue King - Pilot (Principal)

---

teacher professionals all the way to *teacher leaders*. The choices the principal makes in terms of the communications methods and purposes to be employed can have significant impact on the work of everyone in the organization. Along the way, the principal's leadership must shape the view his staff holds about learning itself.

4.4.3 Scholar Contributions

The library media specialist is the person best equipped to observe how purchases and policies are reflected in real life. As a participant in the accountability and learning conversations, the scholar brings valuable perspectives to the leadership conversation, including: the degree of utilization by staff and students; the need for staff development to support professional improvement plans; the adequacy of resources to support instruction through review of curriculum mapping activities.

4.4.4 Leadership Conversations

- What technology applications are most important for all our staff to be able to use?
- What is the skill level of our staff with respect to the NETS Teacher Standards?
- How much time will it take for all of them to reach a baseline level?
- What are the national information literacy standards? How do they relate to ISTE NETS?
- How can we help our students and teachers acquire information literacy skills?
- What are the technology standards for school administrators? Who can best help the administrators achieve them?
- What capacity do we have for our staff to use technology in ways that help them accomplish their goals?
- How can we use technology to minimize trivial, time wasting processes, in order to free up more time for teachers to focus on

development of instructional strategies and getting to know their students better?

- How can we make use of technology in students' homes, in the community?
- How can we help teachers be more productive through technology at home?
- Where can we find the most pertinent articles and publications relating to incorporating technology in instruction?

4.4.5 Leadership Strategies: Powerful Partners

"When principals rely upon their library media specialists to help them guide the growth of educational technology in their school, they can become *powerful partners*. The principal inevitably sets the tone (and leads the visioning process) for a school. Administrators' lack of knowledge about the role (and capabilities) of the library media specialist is a needless handicap. It's one reason I advocate a course involving administrator candidates, preservice teachers, and library media specialist candidates in a team project. Each would learn from the other, and gain an appreciation of the skills needed by the other," according to Janet Murray.

Janet continues, "Administrators need to model appropriate behavior in the same way that teachers do. Administrators who use technology demonstrate that they think it's important to know *how*. We all have to reflect on how learning occurs. I used a 30 second clip of my grandson Brandon throwing a ball up into the air and having it land on his head - three times! - to demonstrate to my teachers that small children do not learn by being told *how*; they learn by trial and error. Some administrators mandate the use of technology and are met by resistance; others (the 'smart' ones) model the behaviors they want to encourage and lead by example."

Reflecting on the strategic role the library media specialist can play, Janet notes, "In a high school, the library media specialist can be a particularly valuable partner to the administrator, because she or he has a more global view of the school as a whole than a teacher who is grounded in a single department. This also applies to elementary and middle schools, depending on the degree to which *teams* take responsibility for entire grades of students. The library media specialist was trained to be a partner to the classroom teacher, to effect the integration of information retrieval with the teacher's curriculum. In some respects, technology is merely an extension to what the library media specialist has always done in schools. Remember when audiovisual equipment and resources were first introduced in schools? Librarians were re-named *media specialists* to reflect their expertise with multimedia, and de-emphasize the traditional association of the word *library* with a collection of books." ("Key Conversations")

The current frenzy about test scores, particularly the disparity between low scoring and high scoring students that grows each year of schooling, can be traced back in most cases to literacy. The library media center is essential to ensuring the highest levels of literacy for the largest number of students. The library media center extends literacy to its fullest contemporary definition, and library media specialists have the expertise to provide "live-in, on demand" staff development in schools where the principal has the wisdom to tap their talents in such a way. As Janet puts it, "I frequently use the term *teaching partner* to emphasize that the library media specialist is a certified teacher as well as a librarian and that I expect to work with the classroom teacher to design the learning activities that take place in the library media center."

These expectations can only become realities when they become part of the principal's leadership strategy. It's time for these important conversations to begin. See Chapter Five for additional resources to improve leadership skills and effectively manage the process of school improvement.

4.5 Technical: Making IT Work for Everyone

Technical decisions can be made only when the previous three required elements (**accountability, learning** and **leadership**) are in place. This means looking at your technology infrastructure in three ways.

- How can learning be strengthened by proper use of the technology you have now?
- What's the life cycle for your current resources?
- What's your plan for refreshing your infrastructure as new educational benefits become clear?

I&T Team Snapshot from Timber Drive: Learning and Software

Frank Creech reports, "We constantly evaluate the worth of available software. Our students are very active with multimedia presentation. We're finding that focusing on a minimal number of programs that allow kids to produce (Inspiration/Kidspiration, HyperStudio, Office) along with certain web-based programs is a better fit for methods of supporting student growth. The value comes from what the students can create with the software they use, not what's been built into the programs when they are purchased."

This flies in the face of other districts, who seem to take pride in the vast number of programs they have available on their server. "We prefer to focus on what students are doing with the software rather than how many types and kinds of programs we own." Steve and Ted agree. "We do our best to keep up with what's available. However it is tragic to see how many other schools and districts are wasting time and money, as if software were a magic bullet."

The North Carolina DPI guidelines for software help inform their decisions. The state, county and district also make available district wide resources, including NC WiseOwl (a collection of Gale online reference and periodical sources), Search-a-saurus and Encarta, so that all students have access to high-quality, evaluated, vetted and organized resources, in addition to what they can find on the Internet through teacher provided links and search engines.

The operational aspects of ensuring that all students and staff have the access they need, in reliable, timely ways, require close collaboration between the district technology coordinator, principal, library media specialist and technical specialist. These are the people who turn your school's technology plan into functioning realities. Guided by the conversations addressed in the first three sections of this chapter, you now enjoy the power of purpose as you pursue your agenda, knowing that the goals are understood and the capabilities you provide will be used for the benefit of everyone in your learning community.

4.5.1 Wizard Contributions

The technology coordinator has overall responsibility for technology at every school in the district. Economies of scale in purchasing hardware, software and online resources have tended to concentrate buying decisions at the district level. Decisions about learning management systems, wired or wireless networking, home-to-school connections, online staff development and a host of other concerns can only work if supported by the infrastructure the Wizard can deliver.

4.5.2 Pilot Contributions

The principal is the only person who can determine where the school lies on the spectrum of readiness for a host of possible technologies. When the principal identifies the top priorities potentially helpful for increasing student and teacher performance, the district technology coordinator and building technical specialist can determine the best way to make these capabilities available.

4.5.3 Scholar Contributions

Janet Murray notes, "As certified teachers, library media specialists see the school network as an opportunity to augment and improve education - for both teachers and students - while technology specialists frequently focus on network performance as a goal rather than a tool. Most library media specialists are dedicated to sharing resources; many technology specialists treat the network as property they must protect. The teacher leader in charge of technology integration can help bridge this gap." ("Key Conversations")

I&T Team Snapshot from Timber Drive

"Having over 1000 logins and over 300 PCs means that the file servers must be maintained and routine directory service repairs need to be made. Other responsibilities of my job include maintaining the school's Internet site and Timber Drive's Intranet site, on-site equipment repairs, trouble shooting, following up on staff work orders (in house or reported to county tech), technology related purchases, providing staff development, assisting in Internet searches for teachers, video taping requests and editing and the morning WOLF TV broadcasts that are led by 5th grade students. So, there you have it, and yes I LOVE MY JOB!"

Ted Fillhart - Hard Hat, Guide
(Network Administrator, Teacher Leader)

4.5.4 Hard Hat Contributions

The technical specialist knows the strengths, limitations and life expectancy of technology resources at the building level, as well as the staff's level of readiness to incorporate existing and new technologies into daily practice. Reviewing data about usage, repairs, software requests, downtime and other quantifiable measures can generate a profile of technology use and needs to guide planning for the current and subsequent budget cycles. The technical specialist will have to live with the infrastructure that's provided to meet the goals that the rest of the I&T team have identified for accountability, learning and leadership, and accordingly provides a valuable voice as a reality check.

4.5.5 Technical Conversations

Technical conversations are organized around three general topics under which are subsumed more specific questions. These topics address present use as well as planning for the future.

Topic 1: How can learning be strengthened by proper use of the technology we have now?

- For what exactly are teachers and students going to need access to the network?
- How will the network be used to support curriculum, instruction and staff development?
- What materials/media/information need to be accessed?
- How quickly, how often, for what duration must these materials be made available?
- Do you notice any changes in the patterns of use among the staff?
- What efforts will we make to reduce the "nuisance calls" (my computer won't work = it's not plugged in)?
- How does our network design encourage participation by students, staff, parents, and the community?
- What do we need to change in order to remove barriers to participation by students, staff, parents, and the community?

Topic 2: What's the life cycle for our current resources?
- What strains on the system will increased use cause, and what is our plan to deal with such success?
- What is the rate of vandalism and what do we need to do to reduce it?
- What is the current average "down time" for machines in classrooms? the library media center? labs?
- What is the best use of the technical specialist's time?
- What is the biggest current waste of that time?
- What security arrangements must be made so that parents, teachers and kids can access some materials from home?
- Who is going to manage/assign/keep track of passwords?
- How will we keep files current, server space available?
- How much storage space will students/teachers have/need?
- Are we going to use a caching server?
- What are we going to do about filtering?

Topic 3: What's your plan for refreshing your infrastructure as new educational benefits become clear?
- What patterns of use will best support teachers? Will they have their own machines, or be sharing that machine with students? Will they work from one location or several?
- What capabilities for audio and videoconferencing do we need to enhance learning (especially for special needs/homebound students)?
- What adaptive technologies will we make available to students?
- What are the implications of wireless networking for extending/updating our network?
- What if students want to bring their laptops in and connect to our network?
- What projection devices will we have available for classroom use? who will manage these resources?

4.5.6 Technical Strategies: "Planning Must Include Classroom Support"

Schools and school districts are still in a development mode for implementing technology in their classrooms. For the most part, they are struggling to find ways to acquire the hardware and software. When they accomplish that, they find out that most of their faculty have no clue what to do with the technology for enhancing their curricula.

It is beginning to dawn on school administrators that they have neglected what would be considered the first step, in any other domain save technology - planning. As *No Child Left Behind* kicks in, many schools and districts have realized the need for a long term technological plan, but most have not yet realized the need for a long term plan for their classroom technology support nor a plan for classroom use of technology. As a consequence, schools and districts have quite disparate services and minimal classroom use, even within the same district.

Exacerbating this problem is the fact that most tech support personnel are working under much worse conditions than they would in a typical business environment. They usually have too much responsibility and not enough time. The good ones find ways to compensate, and still provide high levels of service for their faculty. But many tech support people cope by limiting the ability of teachers to use the technology, and hide the repair schedule and process. The teachers' access to their desktop computer gets severely restricted. Teachers cannot bring in new programs for their student's use without a lot of red tape that removes the incentive. And, teachers have no idea if or when their computer hardware repair problems are being addressed.

Without a written plan for technology support services, neither the faculty nor the administration knows what should be expected, and therefore have nothing to compare with the services they are receiving. A school technology support plan tells all involved parties: what the normal wait times are for specific types of repair, how the repairs are queued, where a specific repair request is in comparison to all other requests, what classroom services can be ordered by faculty, what services are unavailable, what equipment is available for classroom use and what procedure should be followed to obtain any of these services.

At the same time, a plan for the classroom use of technology will tell the faculty: what the principal expects for the use of technology in the school or district's classrooms, which software proficiencies are necessary to acquire and which are not, where to obtain the training needed to accomplish the school or district's goals, and what classroom services can be supplied by the school.

Thus, planning will change the entire dynamic of a school's use of technology. If you want everyone on the same page, you must produce the page to point to.(Greene)

4.6 Conclusion: From the Impossible to the Inevitable

Technology coordinators are asked to do a job that's clearly impossible. It's no accident that it feels like they're asked to do the work of three, because they are! Having a job that takes three people to accomplish makes it essential

Getting Started: Technology - Planning Your Staff Development Calendar

Far too often, technology staff development is too late, too lame. Decontextualized learning ("just in case" instead of "just in time") that teaches tool-centered skills doesn't work for children, so it should not surprise us when it doesn't work for educators. Instead, it is important to anticipate the real work that real teachers will be doing in the near term, and provide experiences, modeling and support that provide concrete ways that technology helps them work smarter.

Now that you've set your priorities, examined activities in the upcoming academic calendar through curriculum mapping, and reviewed the needs of students relative to mandated accountability measures, it makes sense to provide focused opportunities for professional growth that prepare your staff for the tasks they'll face. Here are two great places to begin:

1 What professional development activities suggest themselves as a result of NCREL's "Learning with Technology Profile Tool"? Do your teachers need more exposure to the characteristics of engaged learning?

2 Use the ISTE NETS for Administrators, Teachers, and Students <http://cnets.iste.org/> to guide your development of topics for staff development offerings. Which of these can be best addressed through "team teaching" using the skills of the I&T Team? Can "skills gaps" be addressed through online tutorials?

that we keep our "eyes on the prize" - everything we do must support student learning. This may seem obvious, but wires, boxes, funding, policy, and a host of other priorities can quickly take on a life of their own. Chapter Five of *Information Technology for Learning* is where you can come to refresh your connection to "what it's all about."

Although it is impossible for a single individual to have the skills, experience and talents to do justice to the roles required of the technology coordinator, it is possible to gather the individuals who have these gifts, and work with decision-makers to ensure that your I&T Teams get the time and resources needed to do the job. Yes, the word "impossible" is sobering, but none of us wants to be a modern day "John Henry" as we enter the age of collaboration and knowledge building. Perhaps we can turn this "impossibility" into an opportunity?

In helping you to do so, we've examined each of these roles in context. We've illustrated how to find and work with people whose professional training, experience and contexts are different from your own. We've suggested how to infuse your team with the information you'll need to sustain your influence on the communities in which you work. This will seem less frightening, more practical, and ultimately exciting as you work through the resources in Chapter Five, together! Trust me - the contributors to this book have all "been there, done that" and we know that none of us is as smart as all of us. We've discovered that working together, there's nothing we can't accomplish, and there's nothing more important for us to achieve than the goal of enhancing learning for all students (and educators)!

The educators who share this guide have an unprecedented advantage: the existence of a building level I&T Team with expertise in accountability, learning, leadership and technical issues. This means you can lead improvement from a far different basis than most other schools, even in your own district.

chapter 5

Team Resources:

Vision into Practice

The information your team requires resides in a constantly fluctuating sea of data. In the print version of *Information Technology for Learning*, we've organized resources as responses to questions the I&T team collectively faces. This book also provides you with access to a more extensive updated collection of online materials, specifically selected to support the key conversations we recommend as vital to meeting your school wide goals. <http://oii.org/IT4L/>

Information Technology for Learning: No School Left Behind
Team Resources: Vision into Practice

Contemporary Literacy for the Digital Age

- Expanding Literacy and Traditional Practice
- Using the Big6 to Achieve Contemporary Literacy
- Being Fluent with Information Technology

Accountability: Making IT Work for Assessment and Growth

Hard Data: Examining Student Work
- Data-Driven Decision Making and Accountability
- Looking at Student Work

Managing Student Performance Data
- Learning/Curriculum Management Systems
- Student Information Systems

Learning: Harnessing the Power of IT

Information/Curricular Resources
- Lessons
- Activities
- Websites

Library Media Center Resources
- Literacy, Learning & Leadership

Online Projects
- Free, Subscription Based
- Professional Growth

Leadership: Making IT Work to Provide Sustained Support

School Improvement
- Planning
- Needs Assessment

Policy Overview
- Appropriate Use
- Privacy & Protection
- Digital Equity

Resource Management
- Total Cost of Ownership
- Involved Communities

Technical: Making IT Work for Everyone!

Finding Technical Help

Hardware

Networking

Software

Issue by issue, these are the resources we have found most useful to address the questions of your I&T Team:

Vision

How can we develop a vision for our school?

Critical Issue: Building a Collective Vision <http://www.ncrel.org/sdrs/areas/issues/educatrs/leadrshp/le100.htm> from the North Central Regional Educational Laboratory Pathways to School Improvement site notes that "Schools are likely to be more successful in achieving in-depth learning when leaders work with staff and the community to build a collective educational vision that is clear, compelling, and connected to teaching and learning."

Contemporary Literacy for the Digital Age

Where can we learn how to incorporate **contemporary literacy** *into our school practice?*

The **Online Internet Institute (OII)** <http://oii.org/> is committed to reshaping the nature of teaching and learning by helping educators and students use the Internet to improve achievement in the classroom. OII provides the tools for educators and students to learn, interact and grow in ways necessary for success in the 21st century.

Where can we find guidance on aligning our practice with the potentials for learning in a digital age?

Innovative Classrooms (Edutopia, George Lucas Education Foundation) <http://www.glef.org/classrooms.html> includes assessment, emotional intelligence, project-based learning, school-to-career, and technology integration.

Expanding the Definition of Literacy

The **International Society for Technology in Education** (ISTE) <http://cnets.iste.org/> developed **standards** for the educational uses of technology for administrators, students and teachers.

The **Center for Media Literacy** <http://www.medialit.org/> "is dedicated to a new vision of literacy for the 21st Century: the ability to communicate competently in all media forms, print and electronic, as well as to access, understand, analyze and evaluate the powerful images, words and sounds that make up our contemporary mass media culture."

The **Centre for Literacy of Quebec** <http://www.nald.ca/litcent.htm> explores issues related to literacy, media and technology in the schools, community and workplace.

Expanding from Traditional Practice

The **enGauge 21st Century Skills** website <http://www.ncrel.org/engauge/ skills/skills.htm> describes how high performance school systems embed academic content in skills of digital age literacy, inventive thinking, effective communication and high productivity.

Using the Big6 Skills to Achieve Contemporary Literacy

The **Big6™ Skills** <http://www.big6.com/> approach to information problem solving is the best known and most widely used approach to teaching information and technology skills.

Being Fluent with Information Technology

Being Fluent with Information Technology <http://books.nap.edu/html/ beingfluent/> asserts that fluency with information technology requires three kinds of knowledge: contemporary skills, foundational concepts, and intellectual capabilities.

Accountability: Making IT Work for Assessment and Growth

Where can we find valid, reviewed research to guide our decisions about assessment and instruction?

Practical Assessment, Research and Evaluation (PARE) <http://www .ericae.net/pare> is an online journal published by the ERIC Clearinghouse on Assessment and Evaluation (ERIC/AE) and the Department of Measurement, Statistics, and Evaluation at the University of Maryland, College Park. Its purpose is to provide education professionals with access to refereed articles that can have a positive impact on assessment, research, evaluation, and teaching practice, especially at the local education agency (LEA) level.

Where can we find information about the No Child Left Behind legislation and its effects on schools?

OII maintains a list of resources related to **No Child Left Behind** legislation, research in reading, writing and math, assessment and technology literacy. <http://oii.org/IT4L/nclb.html>

Hard Data: Examining Student Work

Where can we find information to help us effectively gather data, and learn how to use that data to make sound decisions to improve learning?

Examine **enGauge: Data-Driven Decision Making and Accountability: What Does It Look Like in Practice?** <http://www.ncrel.org/engauge/framewk/sys/data/sysdatpr.htm> "More data does not necessarily translate directly into better decisions. In fact, too much information can be as much of a handicap as too little, if it is not used well. Systematic use of data to improve teaching and learning requires leadership, training, and the development of a culture of use. As Mike Schmoker, author of *Results: The Key to Continuous Improvement* (Schmoker, 1999), puts it, schools need to move away from 'continually adopting innovations' and instead 'collectively focus on goals and regularly measure the impact of the methods.'"

Looking At Student Work <http://www.lasw.org/> asks, "Why look at student work? There is a range of purposes including: professional development; accountability (determining the effectiveness of curriculum and instruction); setting standards; and reflecting on student learning and development."

Managing Student Performance Data

The North Central Regional Educational Laboratory **Toolbelt** <http://www.ncrel.org/toolbelt/> offers information-gathering tools (ranging from checklists to surveys) to help educators collect data about their classroom, school, district, professional practice, or community. One new NCREL tool, SeeChange, allows users to display results graphically in order to visualize trends and patterns.

Resources from the Consortium for School Networking Compendium "No More Flying Blind: Using Data-Driven Decision-Making to Guide Student Learning" <http://oii.org/IT4L/lms.htm> include **Learning/Management Systems and Student Information Systems**.

EDUtools <http://www.edutools.info/course/index.jsp> helps educators apply a more rational decision making process to review the many options for a course management system.

Learning: Harnessing the Power of IT

How can we integrate technology to enhance our curriculum?

Skillful Educators (Edutopia, George Lucas Education Foundation) <http://www.glef.org/educators.html> addresses mentoring, ongoing professional development, teacher preparation, and technology professional development.

Information and Curricular Resources

Where can we find our state's content standards?

Mid-continent Research for Education and Learning (McREL) created a browsable and searchable compendium of content standards for K-12 curriculum. <http://www.mcrel.org/standards-benchmarks/>

Where can we find lessons and activities that have proven effective in schools and evaluated web sites that support our curriculum?

The **Big6 Matrix: Use the Internet with Big6 Skills to Achieve Standards** <http://www.surfline.ne.jp/janetm/big6info.htm> links the Big6 Skills to information literacy and educational technology standards, and provides both basic and advanced activities to help teachers appreciate their applicability to research on the Internet.

The **Blue Web'N Applications Library** <http://www.kn.pacbell.com/wired/bluewebn/> is a searchable database of several thousand outstanding Internet learning sites categorized by subject area, audience, and type (lessons, activities, projects, resources, references, and tools).

Kathy Schrock's Guide for Educators <http://school.discovery.com/schrockguide/> categorizes curriculum resources as well as providing critical evaluation tools, assessment rubrics and links to Kathy's presentations and slide shows for teaching about using the Internet effectively.

California Learning Resource Network <http://www.clrn.org> provides reviews of resources to support California standards in English, Math, Science and Social Science. Evaluated resources include video, software, web sites, and CD-ROM. A lesson builder is available to members.

Library Media Center Resources

How can the Library Media Specialist support our efforts to integrate technology in the curriculum?

Resources for School Library Media Centers <http://oii.org/IT4L/lmcres2.html> provides links to sites that define contemporary literacy standards and support student learning through the development of research and information problem solving skills.

Online Learning and Projects

How can we strengthen learning through authentic, challenging tasks that use technology in effective ways?

Electronic Collaboration: a Practical Guide for Educators <http://www.lab.brown.edu/public/ocsc/collaboration.guide/> identifies a variety of collaborative activities and environments, and discusses tools to facilitate electronic collaboration.

The Challenge 2000 **Project-Based Learning with Multimedia Web Site** <http://pblmm.k12.ca.us/> describes an innovative program that harnesses the power of multimedia to engage students in challenging learning activities.

Students complete projects that draw on real-world information and research methods and design them as sophisticated multimedia presentations.

ThinkQuest Programs <http://thinkquest.org/> provide a highly motivating opportunity for students and educators to work collaboratively in teams to learn as they create web based learning materials and teach others.

Web-and-Flow Interactive <http://www.web-and-flow.com/> is a fill-in-the-blanks Web creation site based on the work of Tom March and Bernie Dodge that guides you through creating your own web-based activities for learners.

Global SchoolNet's Internet Projects Registry <http://www.gsn.org/pr/index.html> was created for busy teachers who are searching for online projects for classroom integration.

Professional Growth

Where can our teachers find professional development opportunities online?

Professional Development Online <http://www.ascd.org/framepdonline.html>, sponsored by the Association for Supervision and Curriculum Development, offers courses on a variety of current topics pertinent to using technology in the classroom and school improvement.

The **Distance Learning Resource Network** shows teachers how to find and evaluate online courses. <http://www.dlrn.org/educ/how.html>

Leadership: Making IT Work to Provide Sustained Support

School Improvement

Where can we find a comprehensive set of resources to guide our school's systemic improvement efforts?

NCREL's award winning **Pathways to School Improvement** <http://www.ncrel.org/sdrs/> site helps school improvement teams as they progress through the phases of the School Improvement Cycle.

Subtitled "Change and Technology in America's Schools," the National School Boards' Association's **Education Leadership Toolkit** <http://www

.nsba.org/sbot/toolkit/> provides extensive resources for planning, policy, curriculum, assessment, evaluating one's leadership style, developing teams, planning and evaluating professional development. It includes sections addressing the questions "Why change?" and "Why technology?"

The **National Study of School Evaluation's** <http://www.nsse.org/> current scope of work includes a comprehensive series of publications and services to support data-driven and research-based school improvement planning.

The **Quality School Portfolio** <http://qsp.cse.ucla.edu/> consists of two free software applications that offer schools a solution for collecting and storing student data that can best inform their practices. The Data Manager is a database program built exclusively for schools that enables users to import, disaggregate and report on data. The Resource Kit consists of 21 research tools such as surveys, questionnaires, and observation protocols that can help schools gather data about areas of their climate and instructional practices.

The Northwest Evaluation Association (NWEA) is developing a longitudinal data warehouse of information from schools across the country. The **NWEA's Growth Research Database** <http://www.nwea.org> will contain assessment data that measures individual student achievement accurately and does so frequently enough to capture student growth over time. The NWEA plan is to collect longitudinal growth data from hundreds of thousands of students in order to enable in-depth data analysis.

The **Education Commission of the States (ECS)** provides extensive resources on current education issues. Pull down from the "All Issues" menu bar to select a specific issue. <http://www.ecs.org/ecsmain.asp?page=/html/issues.asp?am=1>

Policy Overview

Where can we find information for education leaders on policy, advocacy and emerging technologies?

The **Consortium for School Networking** <http://www.cosn.org/> "promotes the use of information technologies and the Internet in K-12 education to improve learning. Our members represent school districts, state and local education agencies, nonprofits, companies and individuals who share our vision."

Resource Management

How can we make sure that our plans include adequate resources to address all the costs of supporting our IT infrastructure for learning?

Total Cost of Ownership (TCO): **CoSN's Taking TCO to the Classroom** <http://www.classroomtco.org/> project helps school leaders understand the long term costs involved in building and operating a network of computers so they will be able to budget adequately to achieve their technology goals.

Involved Communities (Edutopia, George Lucas Education Foundation) <http://www.glef.org/communities.html> describes how businesses, universities, community organizations and parent groups can contribute resources and expertise as partners with teachers and students. The community can become the classroom. This site highlights creative partnerships, where technology connects classrooms to the larger world.

The **Baldrige Criteria for Performance Excellence** <http://www.baldrigein education.org/> provide a systems perspective for modeling effective organizational management and performance excellence. An education version of the criteria was created in the mid-1990s as a framework for understanding and improving school performance and student learning.

Technical: Making IT Work for Everyone!

Finding Technical Help

Where can we find advice and information to answer our technical questions?

AllExperts.com <http://www.allexperts.com/default.asp?heading=18> is a free expert question and answer system.

whatis?com <http://whatis.techtarget.com/> is an extensive, all purpose reference. For example, if you search for "router," you will retrieve both definitions and links to manufacturers.

Hardware

How do various products compare?

HardwareCentral <http://www.hardwarecentral.com/hardwarecentral/re views/> features reviews, discussions, tutorials, news and more.

Where can we learn how technology can help our students with special needs?

Center for Applied Special Technology (CAST) <http://www.cast.org/> is an educational, not-for-profit organization that uses technology to expand opportunities for all people, especially those with disabilities.

Networking

How can we make sure our technology and reform goals are aligned?

Networks & Systemic Reform <http://modelschools.terc.edu/model schools/TEMPLATE/Publications/pdf/ElecNetworks.pdf> describes the unique role of networks in education.

Where can we find in-depth information to support network design and implementation decisions?

IT Toolbox <http://networking.ittoolbox.com/default2.asp> contains networking discussion groups, searchable Q&A messages, current networking news items, documents and code, and three networking newsletters.

MAC OS Networking <http://developer.apple.com/macos/opentransport/index.html> addresses all aspects of Macintosh networking.

Software

Where can we find tools and resources for our website?

ServerCompare <http://www.serverwatch.com/stypes/compare/> is the definitive guide to web server and HTTP specifications, and includes statistics on a wide range of servers, including web, ftp, mail and more.

MyComputer.com <http://www.mycomputer.com/> features web tool resources for webmasters including free web hit counters and guest books.

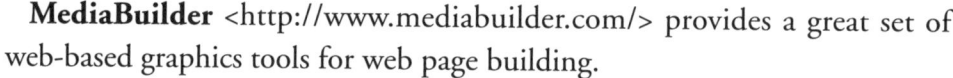

MediaBuilder <http://www.mediabuilder.com/> provides a great set of web-based graphics tools for web page building.

Conclusion

We have a vision: contemporary literacy for all teachers and students will improve student achievement and promote lifelong learning that exceeds the accountability provisions of NCLB. Schools are more than bricks and mortar: their design must be inspired with a view to what will be created and nurtured inside. Our I&T Team has drafted a blueprint to follow in laying the foundation; its members serve as the foremen who provide essential support for our collaborative workgroups. The Big6 Skills provides the scaffolding from which we can assemble the answers to our information needs. The craftsmen who are building our new school are each contributing their individual talents and working at their own pace, but they all refer to the architect's rendering to guide their efforts. Our students are the apprentices who are constructing personal knowledge as they acquire the critical thinking skills that will enable them to succeed in the 21st century.

index

B

C

D

E

Education
  Traditional 89
  Progressive 37
  Transformative 38
educational technology 22, 48, 67, 78, 86, 88, 90, 119, 136
Educational Testing Service 35
Eisenberg, Mike (Michael B.) 46, 50, 51
evaluation 31, 39, 59, 63, 75, 84, 100, 102, 104, 113, 134, 135, 137, 139

F

FITness 36, 95
  See also *Being Fluent with Information Technology*

G

Greene, Patrick 126
Guide
  role definition 72
  contributions 24, 99, 106
  managing learners 85
  See also Teacher Leader

H

Hard Hat
  role definition 73
  contributions 107, 123
  managing resources 89
  See also Technical Specialist
hardware 30, 34, 70, 73, 75, 81, 90, 122, 125, 141
high-stakes testing 59, 96

I

I&T Teams 24, 25, 51, 53, 64, 72, 92, 95, 127
ICONnect 84
ICT Literacy – see Information and Communications Technology
Information and Communications Technology (ICT) literacy 34
Information and Technology Teams (I&T Teams) – See I&T Teams
information literacy 31, 32, 38, 39, 46, 82, 83, 85, 107, 108, 116, 118, 136
Information Power 46, 82, 83, 84
Information Problem Solving 39, 134, 137
information specialist 32, 83
Information Technology (IT) 22, 23, 26, 30, 33, 34, 36, 40, 52, 68, 82, 83, 92, 109, 127, 134
instruction 32, 34, 53, 59, 60, 63, 87, 99, 101, 109, 112, 116, 123, 135
Internet 70, 82, 84, 89, 90, 106, 114, 133, 136, 137, 139
Intranet 70
IT – See Information Technology

T

W

works cited

Anderson, Mary Alice. "Things we'd love to hear more of from teachers." E-mail to the author. 15 Jul. 2001.

Baca, Marguerite. "TSSA: One Principal's View" *MultiMedia Schools*. Sep. 2001: 51.

Baldrige in Education: A Journey Worth Beginning. 2002. Illinois Business Roundtable. 22 Oct. 2002 <http://www.baldrigeineducation.org/overview.ht ml>

Barton, Paul E. *Facing the Hard Facts in Education Reform*. Jan. 2001. Educational Testing Service. July 2002 <http://www.ets.org/research/pic/facingfacts.pdf>.

Being Fluent with Information Technology. 1999. Committee on Information Technology Literacy, National Research Council. Washington, D.C.: National Academy Press. 25 Mar. 2002 <http://books.nap.edu/html/beingfluent/>.

Bete, T. "Who is the Technology Director?" *School Planning and Management Magazine*. April 1998. Michigan Center for Technology Coordinators. 15 Oct. 2002 <http://www.wmich.edu/edstudies/ctc/techdir.htm l>.

Brievik, P.S. *Student Learning in the Information Age*. 1998. Phoenix, AZ: Oryx Press qtd. in Lowe.

Bruce, Bertram and Jim Levin. "Educational Technology: Media for Inquiry, Communication, Construction, and Expression." *Journal of Educational Computing Research* (1997, Vol. 7(1): 97-102) 19 Feb. 2003 <http://www.lis.uiuc.edu/~chip/pubs/taxonomy/in dex.html>.

Carmean, Colleen and Jeremy Haefner. "Mind over Matter: Transforming Course Management Systems into Effective Learning Environments." *EDUCAUSE Review* 37.5 (2002): 24-34.

Clarke, Arthur C. "Technology and the Future." *Report on Planet Three*. New York: HarperCollins, 1972.

Clements, Barbara. "New NCLB/Title I Issues, Department of Education Regulations, 34 CFR Part 200, Changes in Standards and Assessment Requirements." Jul. 2002. Evaluation Software Publishing, Inc. 4 Oct. 2002 <http://www.educationadvisor.info/ocio2001/New%20NCLBIssues2.doc>.

"Closing the Achievement Gap: NCREL Tools." 2002. North Central Regional Educational Laboratory. 14 Oct. 2002. <http://www.ncrel.org/gap/tools.htm>.

Data Connections: Using Assessments to Improve Teaching and Learning. 2002. Institute for the Advancement of Emerging Technologies in Education, Appalachia Educational Laboratory. 5 Oct. 2002 <http://www.dataconnections.org/>

"Develop a Clear, Educationally Focused Vision." North Central Regional Educational Laboratory. 16 Feb. 2003 <http://www.ncrel.org/sdrs/areas/issues/educatrs/leadrshp/le1clear.htm>

Digital Transformation: A Framework for ICT Literacy. 2002. Educational Testing Service. 27 Sep. 2002 <http://www.ets.org/research/ictliteracy/>.

e-Learning: Putting a World Class Education at the Fingertips of All Children. Dec. 2000. US Department of Education. 17 Oct. 2002 <http://www.ed.gov/Technology/elearning/>.

Education Criteria for Performance Excellence. 2002. Baldrige National Quality Program. 22 Oct. 2002 <http://www.baldridge.org/PDF_files/2002_Education_Criteria.pdf>

Eisenberg, Michael B. "Beyond the Bells and Whistles: Technology Skills for a Purpose." *MultiMedia Schools.* May 2001: 44-51.

--- "A Big6 Skills™ Overview." The Big6. 09 Feb. 2003. <http://big6.com/showarticle.php?id=16>

--- and Carrie Lowe. "Call to Action: Getting Serious about Libraries and Information in Education." *MultiMedia Schools.* Mar. 1999: 18-21.

--- and R. E. Berkowitz. *Curriculum Initiative: An Agenda and Strategy for Library Media Programs.* Worthington, OH: Linworth, 1988 qtd. in Lowe.

--- and Robert E. Berkowitz. *Information Problem Solving: The Big Six Skills Approach to Library and Information Skills Instruction.* Norwood, N.J.: Ablex Publishing, 1990.

--- and Robert E. Berkowitz. *Teaching Information & Technology Skills: the Big6 in Secondary Schools.* Worthington, OH: Linworth, 2000.

"eSN Analysis: Technology will be key to schools' accountability efforts." 2002. *eSchool News Online.* 14 Oct. 2002. <http://www.eschoolnews.com/news/registerFP.cfm?ul=%2Fnews%2FshowStory%2Ecfm%3FArticleID%3D3426>

"Final Report of the American Library Association Presidential Committee on Information Literacy" (1989) qtd. in Kathleen L. Spitzer with Michael B. Eisenberg and Carrie A. Lowe. *Information Literacy: Essential Skills for the Information Age.* Syracuse, N.Y.: ERIC Clearinghouse on Information & Technology, 1998.

Gardner, D. P. And Others. (1983). *A nation at risk: The imperative for educational reform. An open letter to the American people. A report to the nation and the Secretary of Education.* Available: Superintendent of Documents, Government Printing Office, Washington, DC 20402 (Stock No. 065-000-00177-2). (ERIC No. ED226006)

Greene, Patrick. "Planning Must Include Classroom Support." E-mail to author. 18 Jul. 2001.

Hinds, Michael deCourcy. *Carnegie Challenge 2002: Teaching as a Clinical Profession: A New Challenge for Education.* 2002. Carnegie Corporation of New York. 20 Sep. 2002 <http://www.carnegie.org/pdf/teachered.pdf>.

Information Power: Building Partnerships for Learning. Chicago: American Library Association, 1998.

Kohn, Alfie. "Education's Rotten Apples." *Education Week on the Web.* 18 Sep. 2002. Editorial Projects in Education Inc. 5 Oct. 2002 <http://www.edweek.com/ew/ewstory.cfm?slug=03Kohn.h22>

Kuhlthau, C.C. *Seeking Meaning: A Process Approach to Library and Information Services.* Greenwich, CT: Ablex, 1993 qtd. in Lowe.

Louis, Karen S. & Matthew B. Miles. *Improving the urban high school: What works and why.* New York, NY: Teachers College Press, 1990. qtd. in Peterson.

Lowe, Carrie. "Research Foundations of the Big6 Skills." 2002. Big6.com. 22 Oct. 2002 <http://www.big6.com/showarticle.php?id=145>

Marien, Dr. Joanne, Linda Chapman, Laura Luke and Elaine Vislocky. "Integrating Information Literacy and Technology Skills into K-12 Curriculum." Somers (NY) Central School District presentation at the National Educational Computing Conference, 1999 qtd. in Murray, Information TeAchnology.

Merrow, John. "Double-Click: Threat or Promise?" from *Choosing Excellence: "Good Enough" Schools Are Not Good Enough.* 1 Dec. 2001. Harvard Graduate School of Education. 14 Oct. 2002 <http://www.gse.harvard.edu/news/features/merrow12012001.html>

Murray, Janet. "Contemporary Literacy: Essential Skills for the 21st Century." *MultiMedia Schools.* Mar. 2003.

---. "Information TeAchnology: Using the Internet for Student Research." *Electronic Business and Education: Recent Advances in the Internet Infrastructure.* Ed. Wendy Chin, Frederic Patricelli, Veljko Milutinovic. Boston: Kluwer Academic Publishers, 2001. 15-31.

---. "Key Conversations: Principal and Library Media Specialist." E-mail to the author. 15 Jul. 2001.

---. "Librarians Evolving Into Cybrarians: New Roles for School Librarians." *MultiMedia Schools.* Mar. 2000: 27-30.

National Educational Technology Standards for Teachers (NETS-T). 2000. International Society for Technology In Education (ISTE). 5 Oct. 2002 <http://cnets.iste.org/index3.html>

"NCLB: Interview with Lisa Graham Keegan about AYP" 26 Jul. 2002. National Governors Association. 17 Oct. 2002 <http://www.nga.org/center/divisions/1,1188,C_ISSUE_BRIEF%5ED_4151,00.html>

No Child Left Behind Act of 2001 (Elementary and Secondary Education Act). Pub. L. 107-110. 8 Jan. 2002. 115 Stat. 1425. 20 Apr. 2003 <http://www.ed.gov/legislation/ESEA02/index.html>

Peterson, Kent. "Critical Issue: Leading and Managing Change and Improvement." North Central Regional Educational Laboratory. 1995. <http://www.ncrel.org/sdrs/areas/issues/educatrs/leadrshp/le500.htm> 20 Apr. 2003.

Pitts, J. et al. "Mental Models of Information: The 1993-1994 AASL/Highsmith Research Award Study." *School Library Media Quarterly* 23.3 (1995): 177-184 qtd. in Lowe.

Preuss, Paul. "Caution about experts." E-mail to the author. 5 June 2001.

---. "A One Page Systems Primer." 2000. Plan 2020.com. <http://www.plan2020.com/page11.html> 17 Oct. 2002.

"Quote Project." 16 Feb. 2003 <http://www.quoteproject.com/>

Ragan, Lawrence. "Guiding Principles and Practices for the Design and Development of Effective Distance Education." 1997. Innovations in Distance Education. <http://www.outreach.psu.edu/de/ide/GP&P/default.html> 20 Nov. 2002.

Ravitz, Jason L., Henry J. Becker and Yantien Wong. *Constructivist-Compatible Beliefs and Practices among U.S. Teachers*. Jul. 2000. Center for Research on Information Technology and Organizations, University of California, Irvine and University of Minnesota. 6 Oct. 2002 <http://www.crito.uci.edu/TLC/FINDINGS/REPORT4/startpage.html>

Reilly, Rob. "The Technology Coordinator: Curriculum Leader or Electronic Janitor?" *MultiMedia Schools*. May 1999: 38-41.

Riel, Margaret and Hank Becker. *The Beliefs, Practices, and Computer Use of Teacher Leaders*. April 2000. University of California, Irvine. 5 Oct. 2002 <http://www.crito.uci.edu/tlc/findings/aera/>

Rockman, Saul et al. "Executive Summary: A More Complex Picture: Laptop Use and Impact in the Context of Changing Home and School Access." Jun. 2000. San Francisco, CA: Rockman ET AL. <http://rockman.com/projects/laptop/laptop3exec.htm> 29 Apr. 2003.

Schmoker, Mike. *Results: The Key to Continuous Improvement*. 1999. qtd. in "Data-Driven Decision Making and Accountability: What Does It Look Like in Practice?" 7 Nov. 2002. <http://www.ncrel.org/engauge/framewk/sys/data/sysdatpr.htm>

Senge, Peter M. *The fifth discipline: The art and practice of the learning organization*. New York: Doubleday Currency, 1990. qtd. in Peterson.

Serim, Ferdi. "Strong Medicine: Scientifically Based Research and School Practice." 15 Oct. 2002. Consortium for School Networking. 5 Nov. 2002 <http://www.cosn.org/initiatives/compendium.pdf>

---. "No More Flying Blind: Using Data-Driven Decision-Making to Guide Student Learning." Feb. 2003. Consortium for School Networking.

Teaching, Learning and Computing: 1998 (TLC). Center for Research on Information Technology and Organizations, University of California, Irvine. 5 Oct. 2002 <http://www.crito.uci.edu/tlc/html/tlc_home.html>

Technology Standards for School Administrators (TSSA). 2001. International Society for Technology In Education (ISTE). 5 Oct. 2002 <http://cnets.iste.org/tssa/>

White Paper: 21st Century Literacy in a Convergent Media World. Mar. 2002. Berlin: Bertelsmann Foundation/AOL Time Warner Foundation. 16 Oct. 2002 <http://www.21stcenturyliteracy.org/white/>

Wiggins, Grant. "Feedback: How Learning Occurs." Relearning by Design. 11 Jan. 2003 <http://www.relearning.org/resources/PDF/feedback.pdf>

DATE DUE

11/17/06			
1/18/07			

DEMCO 128-5046